ISO 9001:2000 in Brief

About the Authors

Ray Tricker (MSc, IEng, FIIE (elec), FinstM, MIQA, MIRSE) as well as being the Principal Consultant and Managing Director of Herne European Consultancy Ltd – an organisation specialising in Quality, Environment and Safety Management Systems – is also an established Butterworth-Heinemann author (see Reference section). He served with the Royal Corps of Signals (for a total of 37 years) during which time he held various managerial posts culminating in being appointed as the Chief Engineer of NATO ACE COMSEC.

Most of Ray's work since joining Herne has centred on the European Railways. He has held a number of posts with the Union International des Chemins de fer (UIC) [e.g. Quality Manager of the European Train Control System (ETCS), European Union (EU) T500 Review Team Leader, European Rail Traffic Management System (ERTMS) Users Group Project Co-ordinator, HEROE Project Co-ordinator, ERRI Quality Consultant] and currently (as well as writing books for Butterworth-Heinemann!) he is busy co-ordinating the establishment of a complete Quality Management System for the Association of American Railroads (AAR) Transportation Technology Centre (TTCI) that is aimed at eventually gaining them ISO 9001:2000 certification.

For this book Ray is joined by fellow consultant, Bruce Sherring-Lucas (AMIQA). Bruce was, for many years, employed by the British Rail (now Railtrack) and held many managerial positions (e.g. West Coast Main Line Special Structures Manager, Eurostar Track, Signalling and Overhead Catenary Realignment Project Manager, WCML Peripheral Structures Database Project Manager).

Since joining Herne European Consultancy Ltd, Bruce has been instrumental in writing the ERTMS Environmental Specification for the European Railways, producing a generic Quality Management System for the UK dental technology profession and Railway Safety Specifications (for a German organisation specialising in railway train control systems). He has also been a member of the ERTMS Users Group Reliability, Availability, Maintainability and Safety (RAMS) Team and is a consultant in MS Office Management.

ISO 9001:2000 in Brief

Ray Tricker

and

Bruce Sherring-Lucas

OXFORD   AUCKLAND   BOSTON   JOHANNESBURG   MELBOURNE   NEW DELHI

Butterworth-Heinemann
Linacre House, Jordan Hill, Oxford OX2 8DP
225 Wildwood Avenue, Woburn, MA 01801-2041
A division of Reed Educational and Professional Publishing Ltd

℞ A member of the Reed Elsevier plc group

First published 2001

British Library Cataloguing in Publication Data
Tricker, Raymond L.
  ISO 9001:2000 in brief
  1 ISO 9001 standard
  I Title   II Sherring-Lucas, Bruce
  658.5′62

Library of Congress Cataloguing in Publication Data
Tricker, Ray.
  ISO 9001:2000 in brief/Ray Tricker and Bruce Sherring-Lucas.
  p. cm.
  Includes index.
  ISBN 0 7506 4814 7
  1 Quality control – Standards   2 ISO 9000 Series Standards
  3 Manufactures – Quality control – Evaluation
  I Sherring-Lucas, Bruce   II Title
  TS156.T74 2000
  658.5′62′0218–dc21   00-049403

ISBN 0 7506 4814 7

Composition by Genesis Typesetting, Laser Quay, Rochester, Kent
Printed and bound in Great Britain by Clays Ltd, St Ives plc

Contents

WITHDRAWN

Foreword

There has never been a time when the demand for quality has been so high! We long ago stopped settling for 'second best' and now expect and demand consistently reliable products or the efficient dependable delivery of services. Out of this demand has come the necessity for manufacturers and suppliers to have some form of auditable Quality Management System. But how can this be achieved?

The aim of *ISO 9001:2000 in Brief* is to provide the reader not only with an explanation of the background, the requirements and the benefits of the new ISO 9000:2000 family of standards but also, at very little expense, to enable organisations (large or small) to set up an ISO 9001:2000 compliant Quality Management System for themselves. The possibility of upgrading existing 1994 certified systems to ISO 9001:2000 is also covered – always with the emphasis on keeping the explanations as simple as possible.

Preface

The new ISO 9000:2000 family is an all-encompassing series of standards that lay down requirements for incorporating the management of quality into the design, manufacture and delivery of products, services and software. The family consists of three primary standards supported by a number of technical reports. These are:

- **ISO 9000:2000 Quality Management Systems – Fundamentals and vocabulary** (superseding ISO 8402:1995 and ISO 9000–1:1994). Describes fundamentals of Quality Management Systems and specifies their terminology.
- **ISO 9001:2000 Quality Management Systems – Requirements** (superseding ISO 9001:1994, ISO 9002:1994 and ISO 9003:1994). Specifies the requirements for Quality Management Systems for use where an organisation's capability to provide products that meet customer and applicable regulatory requirements needs to be demonstrated.
- **ISO 9004:2000 Quality Management Systems – Guidelines for performance improvement** (superseding ISO 9004–1:1994 and ISO 9000–2:1993). Provides guidance on Quality Management Systems, including the processes for continual improvement that will contribute to the satisfaction of an organisation's customers and other interested parties.

To achieve its main objectives, ISO 9001:2000 requires the manufacturer, or supplier, to possess a **fully auditable Quality Management System** consisting of Quality Policies, Quality Processes, Quality Procedures and Work Instructions. It is this Quality Management System that will provide the auditable proof that the requirements of ISO 9001:2000 have been and are still being met.

The main parts of the book are as follows:

- What is Quality?
- What is a Quality Management System?
- The history of Quality Standards
- Who produces Quality Standards?

- What is ISO 9001:2000?
- How Quality helps during a product life cycle
- Who controls Quality in an organisation?
- What are the Purchasers' responsibilities?
- What are the Suppliers' responsibilities?

For convenience (and in order to reduce the number of equivalent or similar terms) the following, unless otherwise stated, are considered interchangeable terms within this book:

- product – hardware, software, service or processed material;
- organisation – manufacturer and/or supplier.

1 WHAT IS QUALITY?

Why is the word 'Quality' (although an everyday word), often misused, misquoted and misunderstood? Probably this is because when most people talk about the quality of an object, or service, they are normally talking about its excellence, perfection or its value. In reality, of course, they should be talking about how much it meets its designed purpose and satisfies the original requirements.

Take for example a £50,000 Mercedes and a £15,000 Ford. It would be very unfair to suggest that the Mercedes is a better quality car simply because it costs more! Being realistic, both cars meet their predetermined quality requirements because they have been built to exacting standards and are, therefore, equally acceptable as 'quality' vehicles. It is simply that the design purpose and original quality requirements (i.e. the level of quality) differ.

So what exactly is **meant** by the word quality? There are many definitions but the most commonly accepted definition of quality is '*The degree to which a set of inherent characteristics fulfils requirements*' (ISO 9000:2000).

Consumers, however, are not just interested in the level of quality 'intended' by the designer, manufacturer or supplier, they are far more interested in the delivery of a product (i.e. hardware, software, service or processed material) which is **consistently** of the same quality. They also want an assurance that the product that they are buying truly meets the quality standard that was initially offered and/or recommended.

This consumer requirement has meant that manufacturers and suppliers (especially the larger organisations) have now had to pay far more attention to the quality of their product than was previously necessary. Organisations have had to set up proper Quality Management Systems in order to control and monitor all stages of the production process and they have had to provide proof to the potential customer that their product has

Figure 1.1 Definition of quality

the guaranteed – and in some cases certified – quality required by the customer. In other words, the manufacturer or supplier has had to work within a Quality Management System (see Figure 1.2 for details) to produce their product or deliver their service.

Unfortunately, with the current trend towards micro-miniaturisation and the use of advanced materials and technology, most modern day products have become extremely complex assemblies compared to those that were available just a few years ago. This has meant that many more people are now involved in the manufacture and/or supply of a relatively simple object and this has increased the likelihood of a production or design fault occurring.

Similarly, the responsibility for the quality of a product has also been spread over an increasing amount of people, which has meant that the manufacturer's and/or supplier's guarantee of quality has, unfortunately, become less precise.

The growing demand for an assurance of quality before a contract is awarded has reinforced the already accepted adage that quality products play an important role in securing new markets as well as retaining those markets that already exist. Without doubt, in these days of competitive world markets, quality assurance has never been more relevant. No longer can suppliers rely on their reputation alone!

Thus the drive towards quality-led production now means that today's major purchasers are not just expecting a quality product but are also demanding proof that an organisation is constantly capable of producing quality products or providing quality services. The provision of this proof is

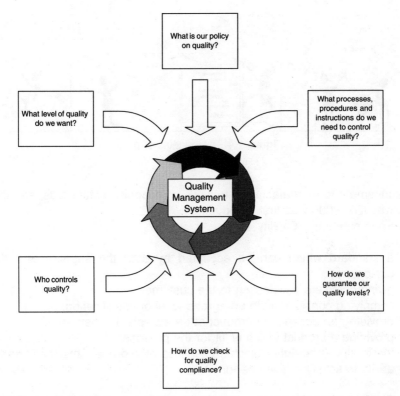

Figure 1.2 Some of the questions answered by a Quality Management System

normally in the form of an independent third party certification and this is possibly the single most important requirement for a manufacturer, organisation or supplier.

Up until a few years ago, however, there were no viable third party certification schemes available. But with an increased demand for quality assurance during all stages of the manufacturing processes, came the

Figure 1.3 No proof of quality . . . no business!

Figure 1.4 The benefits of proof

requirement for manufacturers to work to recognised standards, and this is why ISO 9000 was first introduced.

So in summary, 'Quality' **is**:

● a standard which can be accepted by both the supplier **and** the customer;
● giving complete satisfaction to the customer;
● complying consistently to an agreed level of specification;
● providing an acceptable product at an acceptable cost;
● providing a product which is 'fit for the purpose';
● the totality of features or characteristics of a product that bear on its ability to satisfy a given need.

Quality **is not** about:

● complying with a specification (as it is possible that the specification may be wrong);
● being the best (since achieving this ideal may be very costly and could exceed the price that the customer is prepared to pay);
● only producing a product that is 'fit for the purpose' (as that purpose may be completely different to the customer's actual needs).

Quality is all about customer satisfaction!

2 WHAT IS A QUALITY MANAGEMENT SYSTEM?

'A management system to direct and control an organisation with regard to quality.' (ISO 9000:2000)

It is the organisational structure of responsibilities, activities, resources and events that together provide procedures and methods of implementation to ensure the capability of an organisation to meet quality requirements.

A successful Quality Management System (QMS) relies on a variety of interactions and inputs within an organisation as indicated in Figure 2.1.

An organisation having a carefully structured QMS can achieve their ultimate goals for Quality Assurance (QA) and Quality Control (QC).

The first thing that ISO 9001:2000 requires is for an organisation to set up and fully document their position with regard to quality assurance. These documents comprise the QMS and describe the organisation's capability for supplying products that will comply with laid down quality standards. The Quality Manual contains a general description of the organisation's quality policy and provides specific details about the quality assurance and quality control within that organisation.

In order to be successful an organisation must be able to prove that they are capable of producing the product to the customer's complete satisfaction so that it conforms exactly to the customer's specific requirements and that it is always of the desired quality. An organisation's QMS is, therefore, the organisational structure of responsibilities, procedures, processes and resources for carrying out quality management. As such it must be planned and developed so that it is capable of maintaining a consistent level of quality control.

The 'quality loop' in Figure 2.3 should always be followed by an organisation to ensure that all aspects of the production and supply cycle have been considered in the QMS.

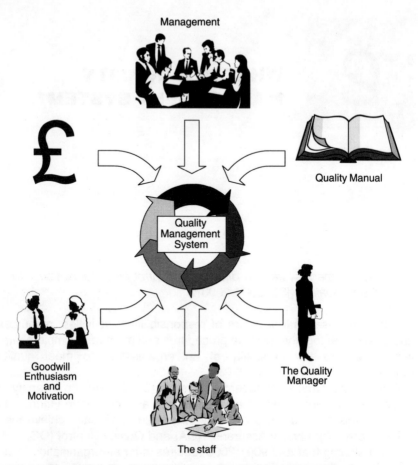

Figure 2.1 The ingredients of a Quality Management System

Although the quality loop suggests that QMSs apply mostly to organisations that manufacture products, this is not the case as they are equally suitable for organisations providing services. So whether you produce 'nuts and bolts', design software or provide a service (such as public relations), a QMS is ideal for running your organisation.

However, to be effective, the QMS must be structured to the organisation's own particular type of business and should consider all functions such as customer liaison, design, purchasing, subcontracting, manufacturing, training, installation, updating of quality control techniques and the accumulation of quality records. In most organisations this sort of information will normally be found in their Quality Manual.

The type of QMS chosen will, of course, vary between one organisation and another, depending upon its size and capability. There are no set rules as to exactly how these documents should be written. Nevertheless, they

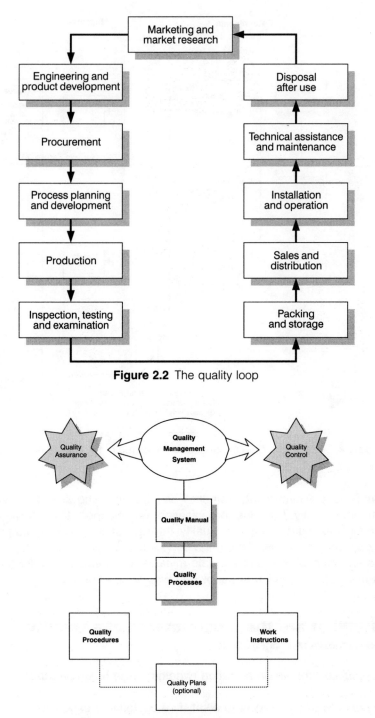

Figure 2.2 The quality loop

Figure 2.3 Quality Management System

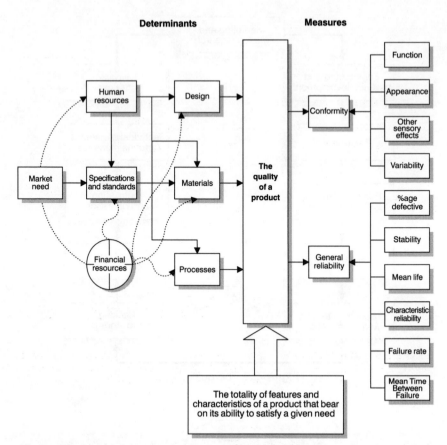

Figure 2.4 Some of the determinants and measures of the quality of a product

should – as a minimum requirement – be capable of showing the potential customer exactly how the organisation is equipped to achieve and maintain the highest level of quality throughout the various stages of design, production, installation and servicing.

As an example, some of the determinants and measures of the quality of a product and service are shown in Figures 2.4 and 2.5.

2.1 What are the requirements of a Quality Management System?

To be successful, an organisation (whether large or small) **must**:

- be able to offer products that satisfy a customer's expectations;
- agree with the relevant standards and specifications of a contract;

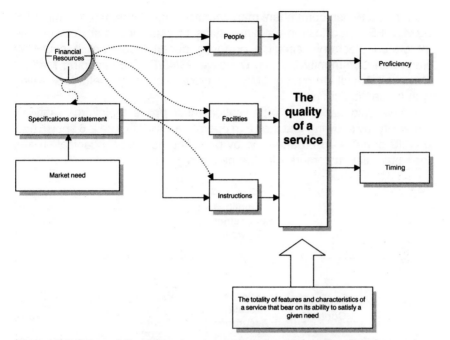

Figure 2.5 Some of the determinants and measures of the quality of a service. (Figures 2.4 and 2.5 are extracted from BS 4778:1979 which has been reproduced with the kind permission of BSI. Although the 1979 edition has been superseded, these figures are included here since they illustrate the concept)

- be available at competitive prices;
- be able to supply products or services at a cost that will still bring a profit to that organisation.

Organisations must, above all, provide a quality product that will promote further procurement and recommendations.

So how can your organisation become a quality organisation? Well, it is **not** just a case of simply claiming that you are a reliable organisation and then telling everyone that you will be able to supply a reliable product! Nowadays, especially in the European and American markets, purchasers are demanding proof of these claims. Proof that **you** are the organisation that **they** should be dealing with.

How can anyone supply this proof? Well, the easiest and most recognised/usually accepted way is to work in conformance with the requirements of ISO 9001:2000. This standard provides guidelines for organisations wishing to establish their own QMS and thereby control the quality of their organisation – from within their organisation.

But it doesn't just stop there! Sometimes a contract will require an organisation to comply with the specifications of other standards. (For example, a British component manufacturer might be required to meet BS 3934:1965 'Specification for dimensions of semiconductor devices and integrated electronic circuits', or for a dental laboratory it could be European Community Council Directive 93/42/EEC concerning Medical Devices.) A well-structured QMS can prove extremely useful for dealing with these situations.

As we said earlier, an organisation must **prove** their 'organisation's capability' by showing that they can operate a QMS. Figure 2.6 shows how a QMS benefits an organisation by providing both that organisation and their potential customers with the necessary proof.

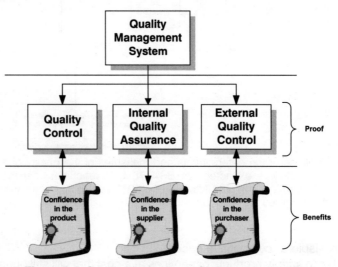

Figure 2.6 Quality Management System – the benefits

To satisfy these requirements, an organisation's QMS has to encompass all the different levels of quality control and quality assurance that are required during the various stages of design, manufacture and acceptance of a product (system or process) and be capable of guaranteeing quality.

These requirements generally cover the following topics:

- organisational structure;
- measurement of quality assurance;
- contract-specification;
- design control;
- purchasing and procurement;
- production control;
- product testing;
- handling, storage, packaging and delivery;
- after sales service.

2.2   What are Quality Control and Quality Assurance?

Quality – *'The degree to which a set of inherent characteristics fulfils requirements'* (ISO 9000:2000).

But what of Quality Assurance and Quality Control?

Although the terms 'Quality Assurance' and 'Quality Control' are both aimed at ensuring the quality of the end product, they are in fact two completely separate processes.

2.2.1   Quality Control

Quality Control (QC) – *'part of quality management focused on fulfilling quality requirements'* (ISO 9000:2000).

It is the amount of supervision that a product is subjected to, so as to be sure that the workmanship associated with that product meets the quality level required by the design. In other words, it is the control exercised by the organisation to certify that all aspects of their activities during the design, production, installation and in-service stages are to the desired standards.

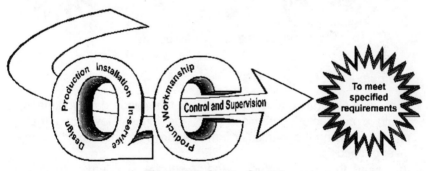

Figure 2.7 Quality Control

QC is exercised at all levels and as all personnel are responsible for the particular task they are doing, they are all quality controllers to some degree or other.

2.2.2   Quality Assurance

Quality Assurance (QA) – *'part of quality management focused on providing confidence that quality requirements will be fulfilled'* (ISO 9000:2000).

'Quality'   is fitness for intended use.

'Assurance' is a declaration given to inspire confidence in an organisation's capability.

'Quality   in a product, by consistently achieving stated objectives, is,
Assurance' therefore, a declaration given to inspire confidence that a particular organisation is capable of consistently satisfying need as well as being a managerial process designed to increase confidence.

QA is also a declaration given to inspire confidence that a product has achieved the highest standards and that its manufacture, installation modification and/or repair has been completed in an efficient and timely manner.

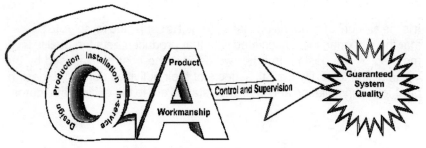

Figure 2.8 Quality Assurance

The purpose of QA is:

- to provide assurance to a customer that the standard of workmanship within a contractor's premises is of the highest level and that all products leaving that particular firm are above a certain fixed minimum level of specification;
- to ensure that manufacturing and/or service standards are uniform between an organisation's departments or offices and that they remain constant despite changes in personnel.

In a nutshell, QA is concerned with:

- an agreed level of quality;
- a commitment within an organisation to the fundamental principle of consistently supplying the right quality product;
- a commitment from a customer to the fundamental principle of only accepting the right quality product;
- a commitment within all levels of (contractor and/or customer) to the basic principles of QA and QC.

2.3 What are the costs and benefits of having a Quality Management System?

'An effective Quality Management System should be designed to satisfy the purchaser's conditions, requirements and expectations whilst serving to protect the needs of interested parties' (ISO 9004:2000).

In practice, some QA programmes can be very expensive to install and operate, particularly if inadequate quality control methods were used previously. If the purchaser requires consistent quality then he must pay for it, regardless of the specification or order which the organisation has accepted. However, against this expenditure must always be offset the savings in scrapped material, rework and general problems arising from lack of quality. How much an organisation benefits from its QMS is directly related to the money it invests. However, it is always possible to put too much money into quality controls. The optimum benefit comes when the investment in quality controls is balanced against the most significant reduction in the cost of poor quality. As can be seen from Figure 2.9, any further investment beyond this point will not result in substantial gains.

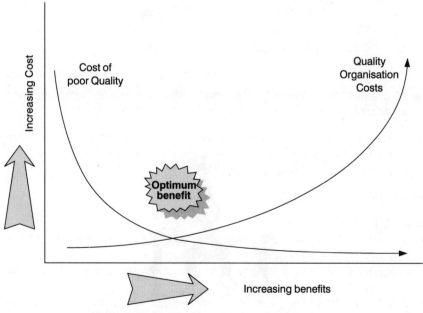

Figure 2.9 Quality Management System costs

The main benefits of quality management are:

- an increased capability to provide a product which consistently conforms to an agreed specification;

Consistent products to an agreed specification

Figure 2.10 An increased capability

- a reduction in administration, manufacturing and production costs because of less wastage and fewer rejects;

Figure 2.11 Reduced costs

- a greater involvement and motivation within an organisation's workforce;

Figure 2.12 Motivated staff are happy staff!

- improved customer relationships through fewer complaints, thus increasing sales potential.

Figure 2.13 Customer satisfaction

For an organisation to derive any real benefit from a QMS, everyone in the organisation must:

- fully appreciate that QA is absolutely essential to their future;

Quality = More orders = Long term security

- know how they can assist in achieving quality;

Why not ... ?

Figure 2.14 How can your staff assist?

- be stimulated and encouraged to do so.

You're a winner with Quality!

Figure 2.15 Be encouraged by the organisation

With an effective QMS in place, the organisation will achieve increased profitability and market share and the purchaser can expect reduced costs, improved product fitness for role, increased satisfaction and, above all, growth in confidence.

But . . . without an effective QMS, organisations will definitely suffer.

2.4   What is a Quality Manual?

'a document specifying the quality management system of an organisation' (ISO 9000:2000)

A Quality Manual is a document setting out the general quality policies, procedures and practices of an organisation. Or, put another way, it is an organisation's written record of what they say and do to produce a quality product or deliver a quality service.

An organisation's Quality Manual is the formal record of its QMS. It is:

- a rule book by which their organisation functions;
- a source of information from which customers may derive confidence;
- a means of defining the responsibilities and interrelated activities of every member of the organisation;
- a medium for defining the level of quality that an organisation wishes to consistently deliver;
- a vehicle for auditing, reviewing and evaluating the organisation's QMS.

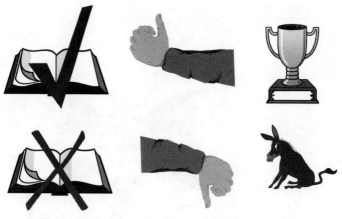

Figure 2.16 A Quality Manual is vital for success

A Quality Manual is the single point of reference required to run all aspects of an organisation to consistent quality levels. It is the heart of a QMS and is essential for anyone considering applying for ISO 9001:2000 certification.

2.4.1 What goes into a Quality Manual?

To be effective, the Quality Manual must:

- include a statement of the organisation's policy towards quality control;
- contain details of the organisation's quality management structure and organisation, together with job descriptions and responsibilities;
- describe the organisation's quality control requirements, training programmes, etc.

The Quality Manual will also identify sub-sets of Quality Processes, Quality Procedures (QPs) and Work Instructions (WIs) and provide templates of the various forms and documents used by the organisation – such as production control forms, inspection sheets and documents used to purchase components from subcontractors.

QPs and WIs will include details of the specifications which must be complied with. For a manufacturer these may include:

- particulars of drawings;
- supporting documentation;
- tools and gauges that are going to be used;
- sampling methods;

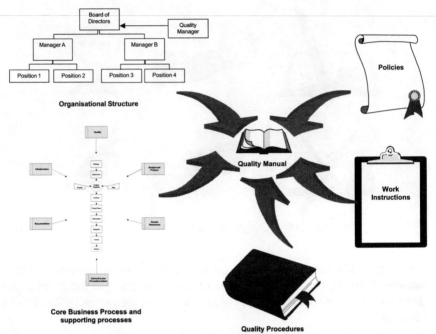

Figure 2.17 What goes into a Quality Manual

- any tests which have to be made;
- test specifications and procedures;
- the acceptance/rejection criteria, etc.

For organisations providing a service the following may be found in their Quality Manual:

- response time criteria;
- service standards;
- customer satisfaction and complaints procedures;
- courtesy requirements (e.g. acceptable telephone manner);

For a complete description and guidance on how to develop a Quality Manual, the reader is referred to ISO 10013 – Guidelines for developing Quality Manuals.

2.4.2   What does each part of the Quality Manual do?

Each part of a Quality Manual has a specific role to play, as shown in Figure 2.18.

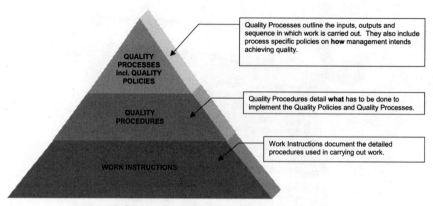

Figure 2.18 What each part of a Quality Manual does

Quality Policies, QPs and WIs are explained in more detail in the following sections.

2.5   What is a Quality Policy?

Quality Policy – *'the overall intentions and direction of an organisation related to quality as formally expressed by top management'* (ISO 9000:2000)

A Quality Policy is a statement of the organisation's overall quality intentions and direction regarding quality (as formally expressed by top management). It outlines **how** management intends achieving quality and dictates how every other aspect of an organisation's QMS is set up and run.

There are two types of policy statements that an organisation needs:

- **Mission statement** – a high level statement of intent from senior management;
- **Process-specific policies** – clear statements of intent for each specific activity.

2.5.1   Mission statement

If an organisation is serious about setting up a QMS, then senior management must commit themselves by stating their policies on quality. Without a firm commitment from top management, an organisation's QMS will fail. As a starting point this is usually achieved by the management putting together a mission statement outlining their intentions.

Mission Statement

Within this company we are totally committed to setting and achieving quality standards that are capable of meeting, in all respects, the requirements and reasonable expectations of our customers.

This company shall develop and maintain a Quality Management System that meets the requirements of ISO 9001.

The principles of ISO 9001 shall be applied to every aspect of our activities.

To achieve this objective, everyone's involvement and commitment is vital in adhering to the system adopted and in fully appreciating their responsibilities.

Everyone connected with this company shall be supported according to their individual needs for personal development, training and facilities.

The Managing Director

Figure 2.19 A commitment from senior management

This high level policy statement should be focused on customer satisfaction and:

- be appropriate for the needs of the organisation and its customers;
- involve everybody within the organisation;
- outline the organisation's goals and objectives;
- be communicated and implemented throughout the organisation;
- be understood by everyone.

2.5.2   What policies do I need?

That all depends upon what parts of your organisation you are trying to control qualitatively.

2.5.3   Process-specific policies

The number of process-specific policies you need all depends upon what activities your organisation needs to control. It may be that all you want to

Figure 2.20 No policies . . . no Quality Control!

do is instil some discipline into your mailroom because the clerks are sinking under a mountain of paper! At the other end of the scale your organisation may be looking to control all aspects of its work. It is your decision, but whatever the reason you must have policies to start getting things under control.

2.5.4   How do I know which process-specific policies to produce?

Fortunately the International Standards Organisation has provided us all with the ISO 9001:2000 standard. This standard requires an organisation to break down its activities into a series of inter-related processes that describe how an organisation manages its quality. Once the Core Business Process and its supporting processes have been identified, it is then relatively straightforward to define policies for each of the processes.

The benefits of having a policy for each process are immense, as policy can be clearly dictated against the main activities of the organisation, thereby avoiding any ambiguity.

QPs are then used to implement these policies and are, therefore, directly related to each process. Any organisation wishing to conform to ISO 9001:2000 will need to have policies for these mandatory elements. These are usually referred to as 'system level procedures' and as a minimum, policies are required for the processes outlined in Table 2.1.

The mandatory policies in Table 2.1 can, of course, be supplemented with additional statements of intent on any activities that an organisation needs to control. Don't worry, however, you don't have to carry out all the elements shown in Table 2.1. You only need to address those that are relevant to your particular organisation.

Table 2.1 The mandatory system level procedures of ISO 9001:2000

1.	Activities required to implement the QMS.
2.	Approving the adequacy of QMS documents prior to their release.
3.	Reviewing, updating and re-approving QMS documents.
4.	Ensuring that the relevant versions of QMS documents are available at locations where they are needed.
5.	Ensuring that obsolete documents are suitably identified (if they have to be retained).
6.	The identification, storage, retrieval, protection, retention time and disposition of quality records.
7.	The managerial review of the QMS.
8.	Training that: • determines competency needs; • determines training needs; • evaluates the effectiveness of training at defined intervals; • maintains records of education, training, skills and experience.
9.	Ensuring access to and protection of information.
10.	Internal audits, which must cover: • audit scope; • frequency; • methodologies; • responsibilities; • requirements for conducting audits; • recording of results; • reporting of results to management.

It is essential that senior management's policy statements are clear and concise. They must also refer to the QPs that detail how the policy is to be physically implemented. An example of a policy on Contract Review (clause 7.2.2 of ISO 9001:2000) is shown Figure 2.21.

Once you've got your Quality Policies in place then you can start adding the 'meat' of your QMS (i.e. QPs, WIs and (in larger projects) Quality Plans). These are explained in the following sections.

Table 2.1 *Continued*

11.	The control of non-conformities.
12.	Ensuring customer satisfaction
13.	The analysis of applicable data to determine the effectiveness of the QMS.
14.	Identifying where improvements can be made to the QMS.
15.	Continual improvement, utilising: • quality policy; • objectives; • internal audit results; • analysis of data; • corrective and preventive action; • management review.
16.	Corrective action, to define the requirements for: • identification of non-conformities (including customer complaints); • determining the causes of non-conformities; • evaluating the need for action to ensure that non-conformities do not recur; • implementing actions determined necessary to prevent reoccurrence of non-conformities; • recording the results of actions taken; • reviewing that corrective action is effective and recorded.
17.	Preventive action, to address the following: • identification of potential non-conformities; • determining the causes of potential non-conformities; • recording the results; • determining the preventive action needed to ensure that potential non-conformities do not occur; • implementing preventive actions determined necessary; • reviewing that corrective action is effective and recorded.

Review of requirements related to the product (ISO 9001:2000 Section 7.2.2)

Policy and objectives

The customer requirements, including any requested changes, shall be reviewed before a commitment to supply a product is provided to the customer (e.g. submission of a tender, acceptance of a contract or order) to ensure that:

- customer requirements are clearly defined for product and/or service;
- where the customer provides no written statement of requirement, the customer requirements are confirmed before acceptance;
- contract or order requirements differing from those previously expressed, e.g. in a tender or quotation, are resolved;
- StingRay has the ability to meet the customer requirements for the product and/or service.

The results of the review and subsequent follow-up actions shall be recorded (see Clause 5.5.7) and the information disseminated to all the relevant personnel.

Requirements

Contract document

The procedure for the initial review of contract documents is detailed in QP/103.

Quality Management System

Contract reviews shall include checks of the existing StingRay QMS to ensure its adequacy. The review may highlight the need to change parts of the existing QMS. In order to control objectives and scope, all aspects of the StingRay QMS shall be subject to the formal change control procedure as described in QP/119.

Scheduled review

The periodic reviews of the QMS (see QP/102 "Management Review of Quality Documentation") and the regular scheduled reviews of all contracts (see QP/103 "Contract Initiation and Review" and QP/120 "Contract Progress and Continuing Review") shall be used as the basis for an ongoing objective to continuously improve the performance of StingRay (i.e. internal management and the conduct of contracts) in order to achieve greater efficiency and effectiveness.

Internal system review

All quality documentation is subject to planned and regular reviews by a Review Team, ensuring that:

- the established systems are still appropriate given any external quality system requirements such as ISO 9001:2000;
- the system and procedures in operation are still effective and remain accurate for the working practices used;
- the data and information feedback from internal audits, complaints, compliments or routine work is considered at senior management level so that adjustments to the systems can be made.

Responsibility

The Principal Consultant has overall responsibility for establishing, implementing and maintaining this activity.

Implementation

To ensure that the above objectives are achieved and to ensure that the QMS is used consistently, the following documented Quality Procedures are used:

QP/102 - Management Review of Quality Documentation
QP/103 - Contract Initiation and Review
QP/104 - Budget and Finance
QP/119 - Change Control

Figure 2.21 An example policy statement for clause 7.2.2 of ISO 9001:2000

2.6   What is a Quality Procedure?

Quality Procedure – *'the basic documentation used for the overall planning and administration of activities which impact on quality'* (ISO 10013:1995)

Quality Procedures (QPs) are used to implement the primary and secondary processes of an organisation. QPs detail **what** has to be carried out to meet the requirements of these primary and secondary processes and their associated Quality Policies. Without procedures an organisation's best intentions will not always be met.

Figure 2.22 Written procedures make all the difference!

Think of QPs as clear concise instructions. For example, management decrees that all problems found within the organisation must go through a problem-solving process (i.e. management sets a policy). A member of staff couldn't be expected to know how to do this without clear instructions. Even worse, the entire work force would have their own ideas about solving problems and further problems would arise because of this.

It is, therefore, essential that all QPs are written down so that everyone knows what to do.

2.6.1   What is the best way to write a Quality Procedure

The old adage that a picture paints a thousand words stands true for QPs. No one likes reading and visually representing an organisation's QPs has

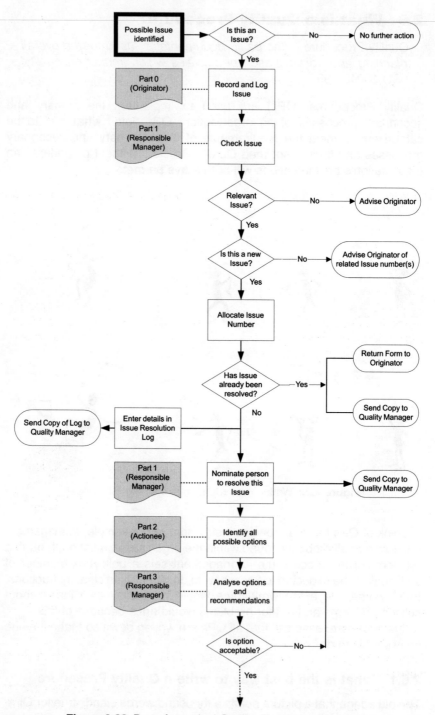

Figure 2.23 Part of a typical Quality Procedure flowchart

always proved successful! Figure 2.23 shows part of a typical procedure for resolving issues (such as problems with providing a service).

These easy-to-follow flowcharts can be enhanced with explanatory text so that the entire process is clearly understood and staff are easily trained. The benefit of flowcharts is that they can be stuck up on notice boards so that the people who have to implement the procedure can readily see what they are expected to do. Ideally they should be coloured for maximum effect.

2.6.2 What should go into a Quality Procedure?

QPs form the basic documentation used for planning and controlling all activities that impact on quality. They detail how an organisation's policy is to be implemented by adding the meat to the process-specific policies. They should cover all the applicable elements of ISO 9001:2000 and detail procedures that concern the organisation's actual method of operation. These will normally remain relatively constant, regardless of the product system or process being supplied.

Each QP should cover a specific part of the Core Business Process or one of its supporting processes, e.g., contract review, document control, audit procedures, training and should be easily traced back to the process-specific policies dictated by senior management.

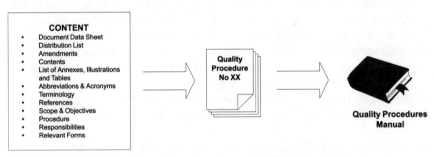

Figure 2.24 What goes into a Quality Procedure

QPs should not normally include technical requirements or specialist procedures required for the manufacture of a product or delivery of a system/service. These sorts of details are generally explained in Work Instructions (see Section 2.7 for further details). QPs can (and usually do) form a large bulk of the QMS and are usually filed in a separate QP Manual.

The layout and format of QPs should be consistent so that staff can become accustomed to a familiar structure. This also helps to ensure systematic compliance with the ISO 9001:2000 standard.

QPs shall cover and include:

- **Document data sheet** – all the salient information about the document – file name, who wrote it, a summary of the contents, when it was approved, who approved it, etc.
- **Distribution list** – a record of everyone who has a controlled copy of the document.
- **Amendments** – a record of all changes made to the document
- **Contents list** – a list of all the chapters, sections, parts and annexes, etc. that make up this document.
- **List of annexes** – all parts of a document should be traceable, especially when they are in separate volumes.
- **List of illustrations/tables** – a list of all the figures and tables included in the document.
- **Abbreviations and acronyms** – an explanation of any abbreviations or acronyms used in the document.
- **Terminology** – an explanation of any technical or confusing terminology used in the document.
- **References** – any reference material that is specifically referred to in the document.
- **Scope and objectives** – this should list why you need the procedure, what it is for, the area covered and any exclusions.
- **Procedure overview and procedure** – this is the main part of the document and details in clear, concise and unambiguous terms the actions and methods to be used. Ideally the procedure should be detailed in a logical order with the aid of flowcharts.
- **Responsibilities** – clear specifications of who is responsible for implementing the procedure and who can carry it out including, (if necessary), minimum training requirements.
- **Relevant forms** – the identification of any forms, paperwork or computerised forms required to implement the procedure.

A typical Quality Procedure is shown in Annex A to this Section. In this example, the QP relates to 'Issue Resolution' which can be traced back to clause 8.5 of ISO 9001:2000 (Improvement).

Explanatory calls out boxes (similar to the one shown below) have been added to the example to highlight important aspects of the QP.

This is a call out box. Keep an eye out for them in the following Annex.

Figure 2.25 A sample call out box to be found in Annex A

2.6.3 Annex A – Example Quality Procedure

Quality Procedure No. 2

Issue Resolution

Version Number: 01.00

File Name: S-QMS-002

Document Data Sheet

This page carries all the salient information on the document

Title	This version	Date
Quality Procedure No.2 - Issue Resolution	01.00	17.12.00
	File Number	No of Pages
	S-QMS-002	15

Author(s)

R L Tricker

Subject

StingRay Quality Management System

Executive Summary

It is essential that all issues (whether technical, management, quality, financial or other), that can have an effect on the overall efficiency of StingRay are first identified and recorded. Once this has been done they can be assessed by the manager directly responsible and referred to the appropriate management level for resolution.

Issues can be originated:
- by an individual on a contract (e.g. a consultant);
- by an individual within a department (e.g. a secretary);
- as a result of a contract, departmental or StingRay management meeting;
- as the result of contractual work.

This summary provides the details of the scope covered by the QP.

StingRay staff may raise an issue **at any time.**

This Quality Procedure is mandatory and applies to everyone in StingRay and shall be used for any issue that can have an effect on a contract.

Keywords

Activity, Deliverable, Document, Internal Audit, Issue, Issue Resolution, Issue Resolution Form, Quality Procedure, Report, Responsible Manager, Work Instruction.

Approved

.... **Date:** ....
(Managing Director)

Section 4.2.3(a) requires management to: *'approve documents for adequacy prior to issue'.*

Distribution List (controlled copies)

1. Managing Director

2. General Manager

3. Organisation Secretary

4. Technical Manager

5. Quality Manager

6. Administration Office

7. Spare copy (1)

8. Spare copy (2)

Section 5.5.6(d) requires *that relevant versions of applicable documents are available at points of use'*.
Note: As computers become part of every company's business (and saving paper as environmental constraints are becoming more of a requirement) quite often only an electronic version of the QMS exists. This version is controlled by the Quality Manager who is responsible for keeping it up to date. Staff can take copies of the server (or company's electronic filing system) in the knowledge that extracted copies are the most up to date. If sections of the QMS are being quoted in contracts the Project Manager concerned will have to liaise with the Quality Manager to ensure that the latest copy is used.

Amendments

Amendment number	Amendment details	Author	Date (dd.mm.yy)
00.01	Draft Version 1	RLT	18.08.00
00.02	Draft Version 2	RLT	25.08.00
00.03	Draft Version 3	RLT	08.09.00
00.04	Draft Version 4	RLT	04.12.00
01.00	First Issue	RLT	17.12.00

Clause 4.2.3(c) states the requirement *'to identify the current revision status of documents'*

This table allows these changes to be recorded.

Contents

Document Data Sheet
Distribution List (controlled copies)
Amendments
Contents
List of Annexes
List of Illustrations
List of Tables
Abbreviations and Acronyms
Terminology
References
1   Scope and objectives
   1.1   Introduction
   1.2   Purpose
   1.3   Scope
2   Procedure overview
3   Procedure
   3.1   Identify issue
   3.2   Issue Resolution Form
   3.3   Issue Resolution Log
4   Responsibilities
   4.1   StingRay staff
   4.2   Responsible Managers
   4.3   Actionee
   4.4   Quality Manager
Annex 1 – Issue Resolution Form
Annex 2 – Issue Resolution Log

List of Annexes

Annex	Title	File Name (if separate document)
1	Issue Resolution Form	
2	Issue Resolution Log	

All parts of a document should be traceable, especially when they are separate volumes.

List of Illustrations

Flowchart for Issue Resolution

List of Tables

Nil.

Abbreviations and Acronyms

Abbreviation	Definition
StingRay	StingRay Management Consultants
QP	Quality Procedure
WI	Work Instruction

Terminology

Any industry-specific or confusing terms should be explained for the benefit of the reader.

Term	Definition
Activity	May concern a contract or venture undertaken by StingRay staff as instructed by StingRay management.
Deliverable	The work produced as a result of a contract or activity.
Document	Includes all StingRay reports, deliverables, and official documents, both hard and soft copies.
StingRay staff	Any individual contracted to work for StingRay.
Issue	Any technical, managerial, financial or other situation/detail that can affect a contract, whether it is beneficial or not.
Report	The result of a StingRay contract, sometimes referred to as a 'deliverable'.
Resolution	The culmination and solution to a raised Issue.
Responsible Manager	The appropriate StingRay Manager or Director.

References

Material associated or referenced in the document.

Abbreviation	Title	Version	Issue date
WI/06	Issue Resolution Forms	01.00	17.12.00

For your convenience, this WI has been included as an example at Annex 2 to Section 2.7, page 47.

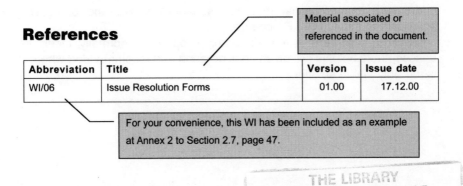

1 Scope and objectives

1.1 Introduction

It is essential that all issues (whether technical, management, quality, financial or other), that can have an effect on the overall efficiency of StingRay are first identified and recorded. Once this has been done they can be assessed by the manager directly responsible and then referred to the appropriate management level for resolution.

Issues can be originated:

- by an individual on a contract (e.g. a consultant);
- by an individual within a department (e.g. a secretary);
- as a result of a contract, departmental or StingRay management meeting;
- as the result of contractual work.

StingRay staff may raise an issue at any time.

1.2 Purpose

To provide a process for the resolution of issues.

> A clear indication of why the QP is needed, what it is for and the area it covers.

1.3 Scope

This Quality Procedure is mandatory and applies to all StingRay contracts and shall be used for any issue that can have an effect on a contract and/or contract deliverable.

This Quality Procedure will also be used where the resolution of an issue is already known, so that the resolution can be disseminated to other interested parties.

Even if the resolution to an issue is patently obvious or has already been addressed, it is essential that all issues are raised and processed according to this Quality Procedure.

General comment – the 'do nothing' option is normally taken as unacceptable but it is still given consideration and recommended where it is the only viable solution.

2 Procedure overview

The procedure is summarised below and detailed in the flowchart on page 38.

1. Identify issue;
2. Record and log issue;
3. Check issue;
4. Enter details in Issue Resolution Log;
5. Identify all possible options;
6. Analyse options and recommendations;
7. Assess results of action taken;
8. Record and log decision;
9. Issue closure.

The following section of this example QP lays down the 'controlled conditions' (i.e. the procedure or process) for resolving issues which, if not addressed, would comprise the quality of a contract (Section 7.3.4 Design and development review).

This QP will also be of use in complying with

- Section 8.5.3, as it is a means of identifying and implementing preventive action;
- Section 8.2.2, as it will provide the auditable proof that the organisation is implementing preventive action.

3   Procedure

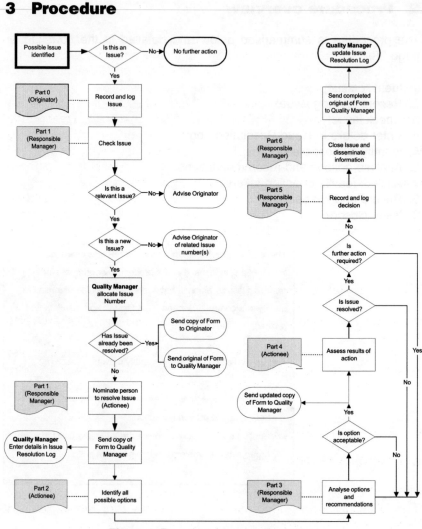

Figure 1 Flowchart for Issue Resolution

3.1   Identify issue

StingRay staff may raise an issue **at any time**.

It is important that all issues are raised, however trivial. Even if the issue has already been resolved or is capable of being resolved by the originator, it must still be raised and addressed using this Issue Resolution Quality Procedure, as the issue may be of use to other parties. This procedure shall also ensure that the resolution of issues is traceable.

3.2 Issue Resolution Form

Once an Issue Resolution Form has been raised by the originator (see Annex 1 and WI/6 – Issue Resolution Forms), the form is passed on to the Responsible Manager who shall check whether it is a relevant, new or related issue.

If this is a new issue, the Responsible Manager shall obtain a new issue number from the Quality Manager and appoint an Actionee to resolve the issue. He shall also send an information copy of the form to the Quality Manager. The Actionee shall identify all possible options after which the Responsible Manager shall review and discuss these options with the Actionee before deciding upon the most appropriate action.

Once the Actionee has completed the issue resolution and is satisfied that the issue has been resolved, the Issue Resolution Form is completed and the information disseminated by the Responsible Manager. A copy of the completed form shall be sent to Quality Manager.

3.3 Issue Resolution Log

The Issue Resolution Log (see Annex 2) is maintained by the Quality Manager.

The Quality Manager shall review the Issue Resolution Log on a regular basis and discuss any problems which may arise as a result of an issue raised and ensure that issues are dealt with in a timely fashion.

4 Responsibilities

4.1 StingRay staff

All StingRay staff are responsible for identifying and recording issues (e.g. financial, technical, managerial or quality related) and for bringing them to the attention of the StingRay management.

4.2 Responsible Managers

Responsible Managers are responsible for:

- checking all new issues;
- delegating the investigation to an appropriate person;
- reviewing the Actionee's recommended solutions and selecting the most appropriate option;
- evaluating the resolution of the issue;
- closing the issue.

4.3   Actionee

The Actionee (i.e. the person nominated to investigate the issue) is responsible for:

- identifying all possible options and providing a recommended solution;
- resolving the issue (when requested by the Responsible Manager).

4.4   Quality Manager

The Quality Manager is responsible for:

- the issue and control of this Quality Procedure;
- ensuring that it is regularly reviewed and updated;
- allocating new Issue Numbers;
- maintaining the Issue Resolution Log;
- maintaining a database of Keywords and previously resolved issues;
- ensuring that regular internal quality audits that address the continued applicability of this procedure are scheduled and completed.

Annex 1 – Issue Resolution Form

Department:		Issue No:	

Part 0: Record and Log Issue (to be completed by the Originator)

Raised by:		Date:	
Target resolution date:		Priority:	

Description of Issue:

Possible consequences:

Supporting documentation attached : **YES/NO**   Continued : **YES/NO**

Part 1: Check Issue (to be completed by the Responsible Manager)

Is this a new Issue: **YES/NO**

If NO:

Related Issue number(s):	
Key words:	

If YES:

Actionee:		
Date actioned/allocated task:		Target completion date:

Details entered in Issue Resolution Log: **YES/NO**

Key words:

Remarks:

Part 2: Identify All possible options (to be completed by the Actionee)

Option(s):

Part 2 (cont):

Recommended option(s):

Affects:

Supporting documentation: YES/NO

Options assessment required: YES/NO

Part 3: Analyse options and recommendations (to be completed by the Responsible Manager)

Agreed option:

Target date:

Part 4: Assess results of action (to be completed by the Actionee)

Assessment:

Recommended further action:

Recommended distribution:

Part 5: Record and log decision (to be completed by the Responsible Manager)

Has the Issue been satisfactorily resolved: YES/NO

If 'NO', details of further action required:

Outcome:

Part 6: Issue Closure (to be completed by the Responsible Manager)

Signature:		Date:	

Dissemination of Information:

Annex 2 – Issue Resolution Log

Issue No	Description of Issue	Date Raised	Raised By	Priority	Actionee	Target Date	Date Closed

2.7   What is a Work Instruction?

A Work Instructions (WIs) provides the 'nitty gritty' detail required to carry out a specific job in an exact manner and to a predetermined standard. They detail how an organisation manufactures a product or supplies a process or service, and the controls that it has in place to ensure the quality of that product is consistent.

Figure 2.26 Written instructions should leave no room for error

WIs describe, in detail, procedures such as 'what is to be done', 'who should do it', 'when it should be done', 'what supplies, services and equipment are to be used' and 'what criteria have to be satisfied'. These WIs should be regularly reviewed for their continuing acceptability, validity and effectiveness.

Inferior or poor design, ambiguous specifications, incomplete or inaccurate WIs and methods, non-conformance etc. are the most frequent causes of defects during manufacture or the delivery of a process or service. In order that management can be sure that everything is being carried out under the strictest of controlled conditions, it is crucial that all WIs (in fact any written instruction) are clear, accurate and fully documented.

Good WIs avoid confusion, show exactly what work has to be done or what services are to be provided. They also delegate authority and responsibility.

Without a written guide, differences in policies and procedures can easily arise and these variations can result in confusion and uncertainty.

As BSI reminds us, *'Instructions provide direction to various levels of personnel. They also provide criteria for assessing the effectiveness of control and the quality of the material, ensure uniformity of understanding, performance and continuity when personnel changes occur. They provide the basis for control, evaluation and review.'*

2.7.1   What should go into a Work Instruction?

In summary a WI should, as a minimum, contain:

● **Document data sheet** – all the salient information about the document – file name, who wrote it, a summary of the contents, when it was approved, who approved it, etc.

- **Distribution list** – a record of everyone who has a controlled copy of the document.
- **Amendments** – a record of all changes made to the document
- **Contents list** – a list of all the chapters, sections, parts and annexes etc. making up this document.
- **List of annexes** – all parts of a document should be traceable, especially when they are in separate volumes.
- **List of illustrations/tables** – a list of all the figures and tables included in the document.
- **Abbreviations and Acronyms** – an explanation of any abbreviations or acronyms used in the document.
- **Terminology** – an explanation of any technical or confusing terminology used in the document.
- **References** – any reference material that is specifically referred to in the document.
- **Scope and objectives** – this should define exactly what the WI is needed for. Normally this is a very simple statement because a Work Instruction would normally be limited to one process (e.g. this Work Instruction details the actions to be taken to dig a square hole).
- **Procedure** – this will state the manner of production, installation or application where the absence of such controls would adversely affect quality (e.g. the hole shall be dug using hand shovels only and be temporarily shored to prevent collapse). Consideration should also be given to any safety implications that may exist when carrying out the process;

- Document Data Sheet
- Distribution List
- Amendments
- Contents
- List of Annexes, Illustrations and Tables
- Abbreviations & Acronyms
- Terminology
- References
- Scope & Objectives
- Procedure
- Responsibility
- Relevant Forms

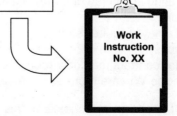

Figure 2.27 What goes into a Work Instruction?

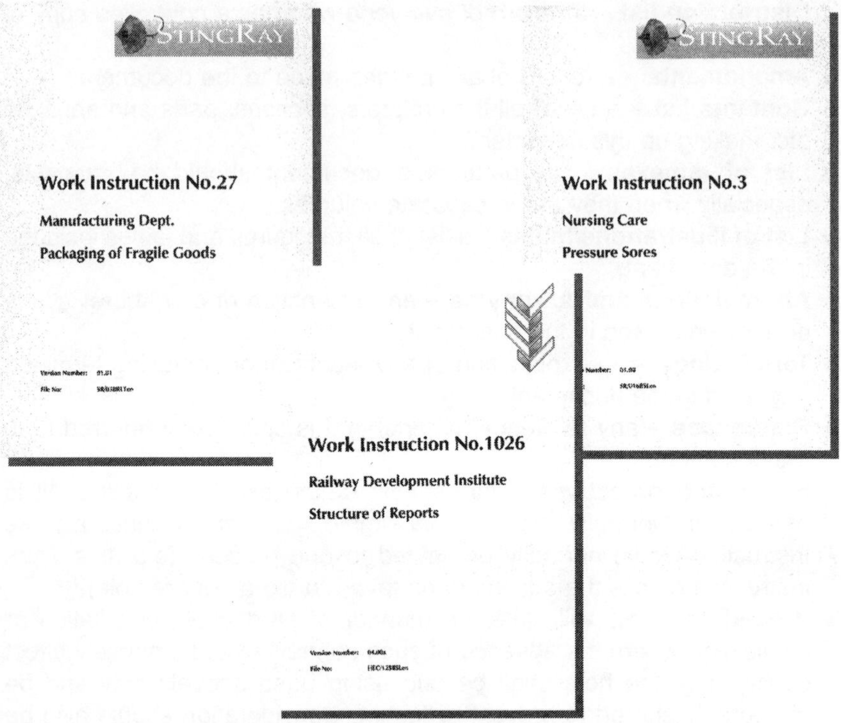

Work Instruction No.27

Manufacturing Dept.

Packaging of Fragile Goods

Version Number: 01.01
File No: SR/63RR Ton

Work Instruction No.3

Nursing Care

Pressure Sores

Number: 01.02
SR/5YsRScm

Work Instruction No.1026

Railway Development Institute

Structure of Reports

Version Number: 04.00a
File No: HEO\2SRSLen

Figure 2.28 Examples of Work Instructions

- **Responsibility** – the WI must clearly state who can carry out the process;
- **Relevant forms** – the identification of forms, paperwork or computerised forms required to implement the WI.

2.7.2   How many Work Instructions can I have?

The manufacture of a device or the delivery of a process or service may require the completion of more than one WI. It is perfectly acceptable, indeed desirable, to separate processes into a number of WIs because:

- it would be very difficult to write a single WI for large items, such as manufacturing an aircraft or laying on the catering services for the Royal Tournament;
- each WI may require staff with different levels of training and qualifications;
- a particular contract may only require the completion of certain WIs;
- small concise WIs are more easily revised.

A typical WI is shown at Annex 2 to this Section and relates to the QP described in Annex 1 to 2.6 (i.e. Issue Resolution).

2.7.3 Annex 2 – Example Work Instruction

Work Instruction No. 6

Issue Resolution Forms

Version Number: 01.00

File Name: S-QMS-004

Document Data Sheet

This page carries all the salient information on the document

Title	This version	Date
Work Instruction No.6 - Issue Resolution Forms	**01.00**	**17.12.00**
	File Number	No of Pages
	S-QMS-004	**17**

Author(s)

R L Tricker

Subject

StingRay Quality Management System

Executive Summary

All issues (whether managerial, technical, quality, financial, or other) that can have an effect on the overall efficiency of StingRay shall be identified and recorded on an Issue Resolution Form.

WI/06 gives guidance on the completion of this form and should be read in conjunction with QP02 - Issue Resolution.

This summary provides the details of the scope covered by the WI.

Keywords

Issue Resolution Form

Section 4.2.3(a) requires each WI to be approved prior to issue.

Approved

.... Date: ....
                (Managing Director)

Distribution List (controlled copies)

1. Managing Director

2. General Manager

3. Organisation Secretary

4. Technical Manager

5. Quality Manager

6. Administration Office

7. Spare copy (1)

8. Spare copy (2)

> Section 4.2.3(d) requires *'that relevant versions of applicable documents are available at points of use'*.

Amendments

Amendment number	Amendment details	Author	Date (dd.mm.yy)
00.01	Draft Version 1	RLT	18.08.00
00.02	Draft Version 2	RLT	25.08.00
00.03	Draft Version 3	RLT	08.09.00
00.04	Draft Version 4	RLT	04.12.00
01.00	First Issue	RLT	17.12.00

Section 4.2.3(c) states the requirement 'to identify the current revision status of documents'

This table allows these changes to be recorded.

Contents

List of Annexes

Annex	Title	File Name (if separate document)
1	Issue Resolution Form	
2	Issue Resolution Log	

All parts of a document should be traceable, especially when they are separate volumes.

Abbreviations and Acronyms

Abbreviation	Definition
StingRay	StingRay Management Consultants
QP	Quality Procedure
WI	Work Instruction

Terminology

Any industry-specific or confusing terms should be explained for the benefit of the reader.

Term	Definition
Activity	May concern a contract or venture undertaken by StingRay staff as instructed by StingRay management.
Deliverable	The work produced as a result of a contract or activity.
Document	Includes all StingRay reports, deliverables, and official documents, both hard and soft copies.
StingRay staff	Any individual contracted to work for StingRay.
Issue	Any technical, managerial, financial or other situation/detail that can affect a contract, whether it is beneficial or not.
Report	The result of a StingRay contract, sometimes referred to as a 'deliverable'.
Resolution	The culmination and solution to a raised Issue.
Responsible Manager	The appropriate StingRay Manager or Director.

References

Material associated or referenced in the document.

Abbreviation	Title	Version	Issue date
QP/2	Issue Resolution	01.00	17.12.00

For your convenience, this has been included as an example at Annex 1 to 2.6, page 29

1   Scope and objectives

All issues (whether managerial, technical, quality, financial, or other) that can have an effect on the overall efficiency of StingRay shall be identified and recorded on an Issue Resolution Form.

WI/6 gives guidance on the completion of this form and should be read in conjunction with QP/2 – Issue Resolution.

1   Procedure – completing the Issue Resolution Form

2.1   Record and log Issue – Part 0

Department:		Issue No:	
Part 0: Record Log Issue (to be completed by the Originator)			
Raised by:		Date:	
Target resolution date:		Priority:	
Description of Issue:			
Possible consequences:			
Supporting documentation attached : **YES/NO** Continued : **YES/NO**			

Part 0 of the Issue Resolution Form (Annex 1; page 60) shall be completed by the originator as follows:

- **Department:** The department to which the originator is attached.
- **Issue No:** To be completed by the Quality Manager once it has been established that this is a new issue (see paragraph 2.2 of this WI).
- **Raised by:** The name of the originator and his role/affiliation to the department or contract.
- **Date:** The date on which the issue was raised.
- **Target resolution date:** This is a target date (set by the originator) by which an issue should be resolved.
- **Priority:** Each issue shall be allocated (by the originator) one of the following priority categories:

  - **Low:** Resolution of the issue is desirable, but not essential at this time;
  - **Medium:** The issue must be resolved, but not immediately;
  - **High:** This issue shall have a major impact on the project unless it is resolved immediately.

- **Description of Issue and possible consequences:** This must be a full description so as to enable all of the relevant parties to fully understand the issue. If necessary a continuation sheet may be used and supporting documentation can be attached to the form. If this occurs, a list of attachments, (including references if applicable), should be added to the 'Description' part and the relevant 'Yes/No' boxes crossed. The possible consequences of an issue (if known) should also be detailed.

2.2 Check issue – Part 1

Part 1: Check Issue (to be completed by the Responsible Manager)			
Is this a new Issue: YES/NO			
If NO:			
Related Issue number(s):			
Key words:			
If YES:			
Actionee:			
Date actioned/allocated task:		Target completion date:	
Details entered in Issue Resolution Log: YES/NO			
Key words:			
Remarks:			

This part shall be completed by the Responsible Manager as follows:

- **Is this a relevant issue:** The Responsible Manager shall determine whether this is an existing or potential problem. If he considers that the issue requires further investigation he shall proceed to the next stage. If, however, he considers that this is not a relevant issue, he shall return the form to the originator together with a suitable explanation.
- **Is this a new Issue:** The Responsible Manager shall check whether the issue has been raised previously.

Where an issue has been raised previously then the Responsible Manager shall enter details of the **Related Issue** (Resolution Form) **number(s)** and any relevant **Keywords** and return the updated Issue Resolution Form to the originator with any relevant information.

If this is a new issue it shall be allocated an Issue Number (which shall be placed at the top of the Issue Resolution Form) by the Quality Manager.

The Quality Manager shall record the details in the in the Issue Resolution Log (Annex 2; page 62) which shall be maintained by him.

The Responsible Manager shall complete the remainder of this part of the form as follows:

- **Actionee:** The Responsible Manager shall decide on an appropriate person to resolve the issue.
- **Date actioned/allocated task:** The date on which the person was actioned (or allocated) to complete the task.
- **Target completion date:** This is normally the target date set by the originator (see Part 0) by which the issue should be resolved. If there is a difference between the dates then an appropriate note should be included in the **Remarks** part of this part.
- **Details entered in Issue Resolution Log:** This is a check (reminder) that the issue has been appropriately recorded for future reference by the Quality Manager.
- **Keywords:** The appropriate key words about the issue shall be entered here.
- **Remarks:** If the issue has already been resolved and the form has been raised to ensure its dissemination to other parties, the Responsible Manager makes the appropriate note in this part and returns it to the originator with instructions on how best to disseminate the information. Reasons for allocating this task a different **Target completion date** may also be recorded here.

An information copy of the Issue Resolution Form shall be sent to the Quality Manager.

2.3   Identify all possible options – Part 2

Part 2: Identify All possible options (to be completed by the Actionee)
Option(s):
Option(s) recommended:
Effects:
Supporting documentation: **YES/NO**
Options assessment required: **YES/NO**

Part 2 shall be completed by the Actionee to resolve the issue.

The Responsible Manager shall task the Actionee with finding all possible options to resolve the specific issue together with an indication of their relative merits.

The Actionee shall identify the possible options to resolve the issue. (It may be necessary for the Actionee to research the issue in order to generate a number of options.) The Actionee then completes Part 2 as follows:

- **Option(s):** This must be a complete listing of all possible options that are available to resolve the issue.
- **Option(s) recommended:** The Actionee's recommended option(s) to resolve the issue.
- **Effects:** Complete details of all the effects caused by implementing the option(s) to resolve the issue. This may possibly include a list of documents, Quality Procedures or Work Instructions that need to be altered, reports that need to be updated or deliverables that require amendment, etc.
- **Supporting documentation:** An indicator to show that supporting documentation has been attached to the Issue Resolution Form.
- **Option assessment required:** To show whether further evaluation of the option(s) is required.

2.4 Analyse options and recommendations – Part 3

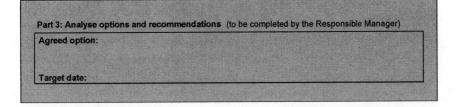

The Responsible Manager completes Part 3 as follows:

- **Agreed option:** The Responsible Manager shall review and discuss all the possible options with the Actionee and select the most appropriate option. The Actionee is responsible for carrying out the action to resolve the issue, whether directly or indirectly through delegation.
- The Responsible Manager shall use the criteria developed at this stage as the basis for the later decision as to whether or not the issue has been fully resolved. It is essential, therefore, that both parties fully understand what is required.
- **Target date:** The date (set by the Responsible Manager) for completion of the action to resolve the issue.

2.5   Assess results of action taken – Part 4

Part 4: Assess results of action (to be completed by the Actionee)

Assessment:
Recommended further action:
Recommended distribution:

When the Actionee is satisfied that the issue is resolved and all necessary actions have been carried out, he completes Part 4 of the Issue Resolution Form as follows:

- **Assessment:** This part should be used to briefly describe how the issue has been resolved. If attachments are supplied, these should be listed in this part (including references if applicable). This part should also include the rationale for the chosen option and a list of the outputs produced as a result of resolving the issue.
- **Recommended further action:** Details of any further or future actions that are required in order to finalise this issue.
- **Recommended distribution:** The Actionee may, where appropriate, recommend to whom the issue should be distributed.

2.6   Record and log decision – Part 5

Part 5: Record and log decision (to be completed by the Responsible Manager)

Has the Issue been satisfactorily resolved: YES/NO
If "NO", details of further action required:
Outcome:

The Responsible Manager shall complete Part 5 as follows:

- **Has issue been satisfactorily resolved Yes/No:** The Responsible Manager shall make a judgement as to whether or not the issue has been satisfactorily resolved.
- **If 'No' – Details of further action required:** If it is decided that the issue is not satisfactorily resolved then the relevant points shall be discussed with the Actionee to assess what further action needs to be taken in order to resolve the issue.
- **Outcome:** The details of the decision shall be filled in on the Issue Resolution Form on completion of the action. If completion is satisfactory then it can be signed off.

1.7   Issue closure – Part 6

Part 6: Issue Closure (to be completed by the Responsible Manager)		
Signature:	Date:	
Dissemination of Information:		

The Responsible Manager shall complete Part 6 as follows:

- **Signature and Date:** When the Responsible Manager is satisfied that the issue is completed satisfactorily, it shall be signed off. The Responsible Manager shall sign and date the Issue Resolution Form in Part 6 to indicate that the issue is now closed.
- **Dissemination of the decision:** The decision shall be disseminated to members of the sector and any other relevant parties.

The Responsible Manager shall send the completed Issue Resolution Form, plus any attachments, to the Quality Manager.

The Quality Manager shall complete the Date Closed in the Issue Resolution Log. The original of the Issue Resolution Form shall then be filed in the Issue Resolution Log and the copy of the form already in the log shall be destroyed.

Annex 1 – Issue Resolution Form

Department:		Issue No:	

Part 0: Record and Log Issue (to be completed by the Originator)

Raised by:		Date:	
Target resolution date:		Priority:	

Description of Issue:

Possible consequences:

Supporting documentation attached : **YES/NO**   Continued : **YES/NO**

Part 1: Check Issue (to be completed by the Responsible Manager)

Is this a new Issue: YES/NO		
If NO:		
Related Issue number(s):		
Key words:		
If YES:		
Actionee:		
Date actioned/allocated task:	Target completion date:	

Details entered in Issue Resolution Log: YES/NO

Key words:

Remarks:

Part 2: Identify All possible options (to be completed by the Actionee)

Option(s):

Part 2 (cont):

Recommended option(s):
Affects:
Supporting documentation: YES/NO
Options assessment required: YES/NO

Part 3: Analyse options and recommendations (to be completed by the Responsible Manager)

Agreed option:
Target date:

Part 4: Assess results of action (to be completed by the Actionee)

Assessment:
Recommended further action:
Recommended distribution:

Part 5: Record and log decision (to be completed by the Responsible Manager)

Has the Issue been satisfactorily resolved: YES/NO
If 'NO', details of further action required:
Outcome:

Part 6: Issue Closure (to be completed by the Responsible Manager)

Signature:		Date:	
Dissemination of Information:			

Annex 2 – Issue Resolution Log

Issue No	Description of Issue	Date Raised	Raised By	Priority	Actionee	Target Date	Date Closed

2.8 What is a Quality Process?

Quality Process – *'a set of interrelated or interfacing activities which transform inputs into outputs'* (ISO 9000:2000)

Figure 2.29 What is a process?

Processes can be found all around us. Take for example the process of getting up in the morning. The initial starting point (input) would be you sleeping in bed. The alarm clock would carry out the process of waking you up, which would be followed by the action of getting up (the output). The alarm clock (the process) would then need to have some quality controls (such as checking that the clock is telling the correct time before going to bed, setting the wake up time and ensuring the alarm is switched on) to ensure that the process will work.

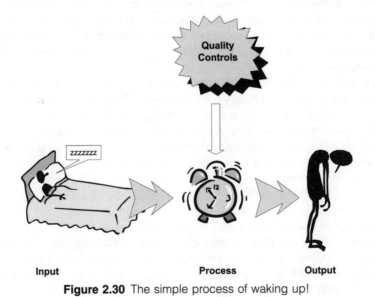

Input   **Process**   **Output**

Figure 2.30 The simple process of waking up!

An example of a more complex process would be building a computer network, where inputs are both human and physical. The method of combining the skills of the technician, the component parts of the system and, most important, meeting the customer's requirements, are controlled by a process specifically developed to deliver an acceptable result (i.e. the output).

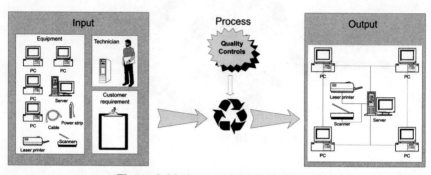

Figure 2.31 A more complex process

2.8.1   The process approach

Any activity that receives inputs and converts them to outputs can be considered as a process. Often, the output from one process will directly form the input into the next process.

For organisations to function effectively, they will have to identify and manage numerous interlinked processes. This systematic identification and management of the processes employed within an organisation (and particularly the interactions between such processes) is referred to as the 'process approach'.

Throughout ISO 9001:2000, the requirement for continuous improvement is frequently (and heavily) emphasised. The process model in Figure 2.32 clearly shows how the four major sections of ISO 9001:2000 interrelate (i.e. management responsibility, resource management, product realisation, measurement, analysis and improvement) and how the improvement processes continuously revolve around all other aspects of quality management.

Each of these four sections is then sub-divided into a series of elements or sub-sections but, the most important element is Section 5.1 (Management commitment) which states that *'top management shall provide evidence of its commitment to the development and implementation of the Quality Management System and continually improving its effectiveness'*.

For clarity, the QMS requirements and management responsibilities can be combined as shown in Figure 2.33.

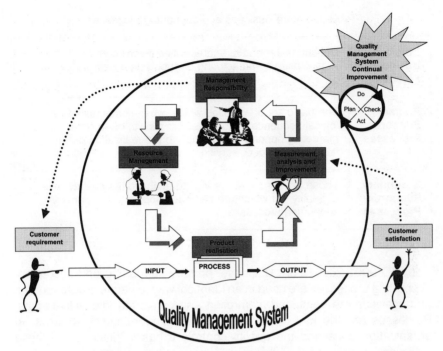

Figure 2.32 The ISO 9001:2000 process model

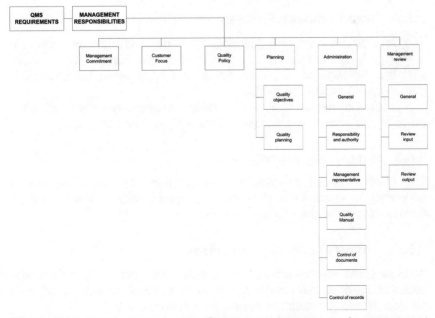

Figure 2.33 Quality Management System requirements and management responsibilities

Table 2.2 Core Business and supporting processes

Core Business Process	Describes the end to end activities involved in an organisation manufacturing or supplying a deliverable.
Primary Supporting Processes	The basic set of activities which, when combined into a logical sequence, takes you from receipt of an order (or marketing opportunity) through to the realisation of the finished product or service.
Secondary Supporting Processes	Those activities that are vital to attaining the desired levels of quality but which are seen as supporting the primary supporting processes

In ISO 9001:2000, Core Business, primary supporting and secondary supporting processes are used in an identical way to define how resources and activities are combined, controlled and converted into deliverables. Processes are the key to providing a clear understanding of what an organisation does and the quality controls it has in place to do those activities.

These processes are explained in more detail on the following pages.

2.8.2   Core Business Process

The Core Business Process describes the end to end activities involved in producing a contract deliverable or marketing opportunity. It commences with the definition of corporate policy and ends when the product is manufactured and/or marketed.

A process owner with full responsibility and authority for managing the process and achieving process objectives should be nominated.

2.8.3   Supporting processes

The Core Business Process is then supplemented by a number of supporting processes that describe the infrastructure required to manufacture (or supply) the product on time.

2.8.3.1   Primary supporting processes

All businesses revolve around taking inputs and putting them through a series of activities that turn them into useful outputs, be that a product or service. These activities are the supporting processes.

A flowchart of a typical primary supporting processes is shown in Figure 2.36.

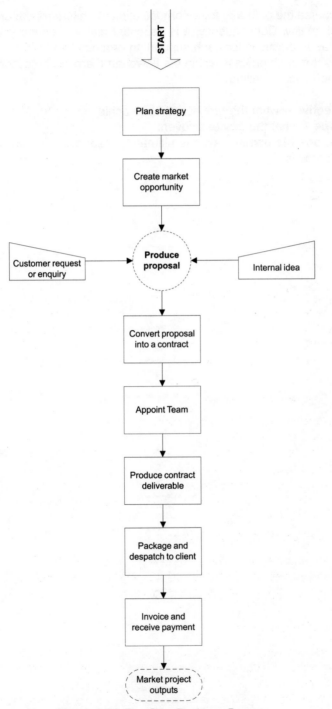

Figure 2.34 The Core Business Process

Of course the only way for an organisation to ensure repeat orders is to control quality. Consequently, it is essential that you define your quality policy and objectives for each supporting process.

Thus, for each process within the flowchart there will be accompanying documentation detailing:

- **Objective** – what the process aims to achieve.
- **Scope** – what the process covers.
- **Responsible owner** – who is ultimately responsible for implementing the process.

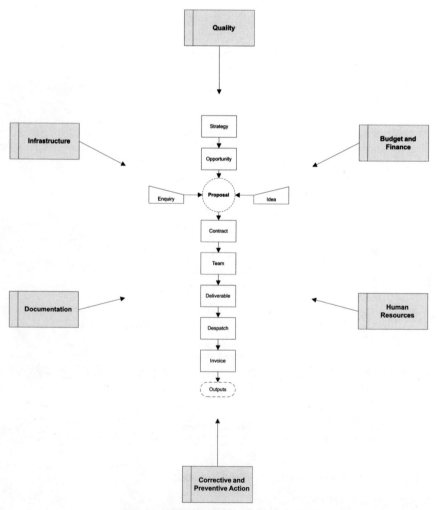

Figure 2.35 Supporting processes

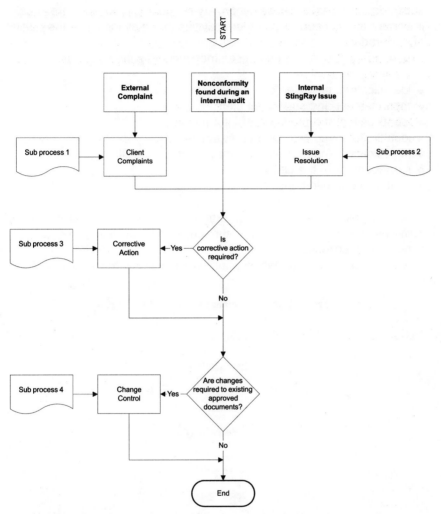

Figure 2.36 Flowchart showing typical primary supporting process

- **Policy** – what the organisation intends doing to ensure quality is controlled.
- **Key performance indicators** – those items of objective evidence that can be used as a way of monitoring performance of the process.
- reference to **supporting system documentation** (i.e. QPs and WIs).

2.8.3.2 Secondary supporting processes

In addition to primary supporting processes there will be **secondary supporting processes** that run in parallel with and support the primary supporting processes. These secondary supporting processes are equally important as they control all other activities that may influence the quality of the product.

Secondary supporting processes may include such things as:

- identification, provision of suitable staff;
- management and support of staff;
- identification and provision of information;
- identification and provision of materials;
- identification and provision of equipment and facilities;
- management of the QMS;
- continual improvement.

The purpose of secondary supporting processes is to document those activities that are essential for supporting and achieving the primary supporting processes.

An example of a secondary supporting process is shown in Figure 2.37.

Identification, provision, management and support of staff

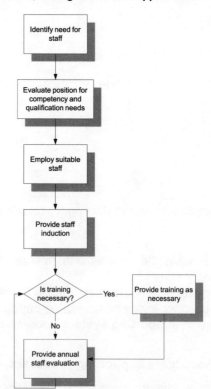

Figure 2.37 An example of a secondary supporting process flowchart

These secondary supporting processes will have an identical structure to the primary supporting processes, and will also have their own associated supporting documentation, (i.e. QPs and WIs).

2.8.4 Inter-relationship of process documentation

All processes are documented to give a complete picture of how to perform the activity to a consistent level of quality. The level of detail varies depending whether it is a:

- **Process** – an outline of its objective, scope and key performance indicators;
- **Quality Procedure** – an enlargement of the process explaining how it is controlled;
- **Work Instruction** – the 'fine print' required to perform a specific activity.

All these documents are explained in more detail elsewhere in this book.

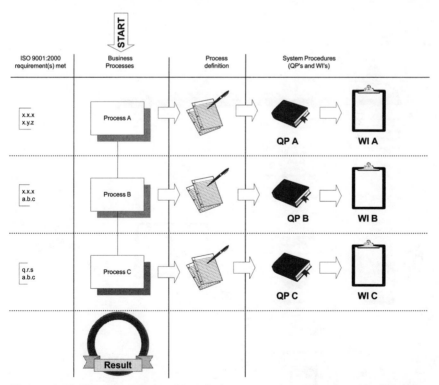

Figure 2.38 The inter-relationship of documented processes with QPs/WIs. **NOTE:** By using a matrix such as this, it is possible to identify the parts of ISO 9001:2000 which are met by each process.

2.9   What is a Quality Plan?

'. . . a document specifying which procedures and associated resources shall be applied, by whom and when to a specific project product, process or contract' (ISO 9000:2000)

Quality Plans are used to record the quality requirements for a particular contract, product or service and to monitor and assess adherence to those requirements.

You may already have quality controls for your normal products or services, but what do you do if someone wants something different? You could simply apply your existing quality controls, but it is unlikely that they will cover all eventualities. What you need is a Quality Plan to address the specific requirements of that particular contract.

A Quality Plan is effectively a sub-set of the actual Quality Manual. Some may even say that it is a 'customised Quality Manual' as the layout of the Quality Plan will be very similar to that of the Quality Manual and need only **refer** to the QPs and WIs contained in that

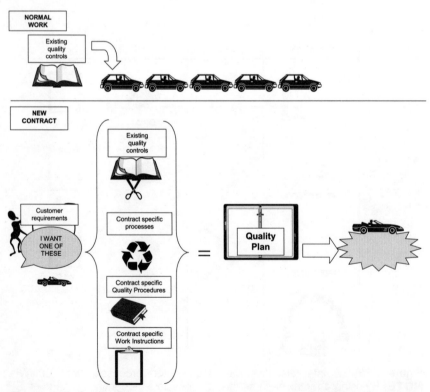

Figure 2.39 Quality Plans are needed to control the quality of specific projects

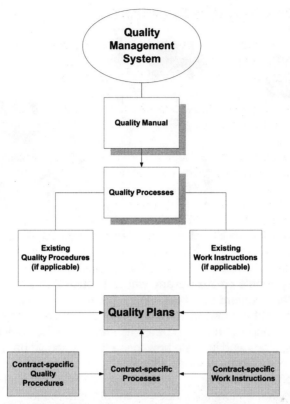

Figure 2.40 A Quality Plan supplements the organisation's existing QMS

Quality Manual. These will be supplemented by detailed **contract-specific** QPs and WIs.

In essence, Quality Plans provide a collated summary of the requirements for a specific project. They will cover all of the quality practices and resources that are going to be used, the sequence of events relevant to that product, the specific allocation of responsibilities, methods, QPs and WIs, together with details of the testing, inspection, examination and audit programme stages.

In addition to being ideal for controlling the quality of manufactured goods, Quality Plans are equally suited to the delivery of processes and/or services. For example, your organisation may provide catering services, in which case Quality Plans would be an ideal way of controlling wedding receptions etc, because no two events are the same.

The main requirement of a Quality Plan, however, is to provide the customer (and the workforce) with clear, concise instructions. These instructions must be adequately recorded and be made available for examination by the customer. They must leave no room for error but

Figure 2.41 The lack of a Quality Plan can have disastrous results!

equally they should be flexible and written in such a way that it is possible to modify their content to reflect changing circumstances.

A well thought out Quality Plan will divide the project into stages, show what type of inspection has to be completed at the beginning, during, or end of each stage and indicate how these details should be recorded. The Quality Plan should be planned and developed in conjunction with design, development, manufacturing, subcontract pre and post installation work and ensure that all functions have been fully catered for.

2.9.1   What should be covered by a Quality Plan?

One of the main objectives of quality planning is to identify any special or unusual requirements, processes and techniques (including those requirements that are unusual by reason of newness, unfamiliarity, lack of experience and/or absence of precedents). As ISO 9000 points out, if the contract specifies that a Quality Plan is required, then that Quality Plan should fully cover the areas listed in Figure 2.42.

2.9.1.1   Management responsibility

The Quality Plan should show who is responsible for:

- ensuring activities are planned, implemented, controlled and monitored;
- communicating requirements and resolving problems;
- reviewing audit results;
- authorising exemption requests;
- implementing corrective action requests.

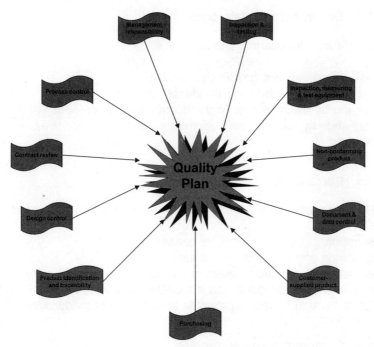

Figure 2.42 What should be covered by a Quality Plan

Where the necessary documentation is already available under an existing QMS, the Quality Plan need only refer to a specific situation or specification.

2.9.1.2 Contract review

Contract review should cover:

- when, how and by whom the review is made;
- how the results are to be documented;
- how conflicting instructions or ambiguities are resolved.

2.9.1.3 Design control

Design control should indicate:

- when, how and by whom the design process, validation and verification of the design output is carried out, controlled and documented;
- any customer involvement;
- applicable codes of practice, standards, specifications and regulatory requirements.

2.9.1.4 Document and data control

Document and data control should refer to:

- what is provided and how it is controlled;
- how related documents will be identified;
- how and by whom access to the documents can be obtained;
- how and by whom the original documents are reviewed and approved.

2.9.1.5 Purchasing

Under the heading of purchasing the following should be indicated:

- the important products to be purchased;
- the source and requirements relating to them;
- the method, evaluation, selection and control of subcontractors;
- the need for a subcontractor's Quality Plan in order to satisfy the regulatory requirements applicable to purchase of products/services.

2.9.1.6 Customer supplied product

Customer supplied products should refer to:

- how they are identified and controlled;
- how they are verified as meeting specified requirements;
- how non-conformance is dealt with.

2.9.1.7 Product identification and traceability

If traceability is a requirement then the plan should:

- define its scope and extent (including how services/products are identified);
- indicate how contractual and regulatory authority traceability requirements are identified and incorporated into working documents;
- indicate how records are to be generated, controlled and distributed.

2.9.1.8 Process control

Process control may include:

- the contract-specific QPs and WIs;
- process steps;

- methods to monitor and control processes;
- service/product characteristics;
- reference criteria for workmanship;
- special and qualified processes;
- tools, techniques and methods to be used.

2.9.1.9 Inspection and testing

Inspection and testing should indicate:

- any inspection and test plan;
- how the product shall be verified;
- the location of inspection and test points;
- procedures and acceptance criteria;
- witness verification points (customers as well as regulatory);
- where, when and how the customer requires third parties to perform:
  - type tests;
  - witness testing;
  - service/product verification;
  - material, service/product, process or personnel certification.

2.9.1.10 Inspection, measuring and test equipment

Inspection, measuring and test equipment should:

- refer to the identity of the equipment;
- refer to the method of calibration;
- indicate and record calibration status and usage of the equipment;
- indicate specific requirements for the identification of inspection and test status.

2.9.1.11 Non-conforming product

Under the heading of non-conforming service/product, an indication should be given:

- of how such a service/product is identified and segregated;
- the degree or type of rework allowed;
- the circumstances under which the supplier can request concessions.

Details should also be provided with respect to:

- corrective and preventive action;
- handling, storage, packaging, preservation and delivery.

2.9.2   Other considerations

Quality Plans should:

- indicate key quality records (i.e. what they are, how long they should be kept, where and by whom);
- suggest how legal or regulatory requirements are to be satisfied;
- specify the form in which records should be kept (e.g. paper, microfilm or disc);
- define liability, storage, retrievability, disposition and confidentiality requirements;
- include the nature and extent of quality audits to be undertaken;
- indicate how the audit results are to be used to correct and prevent recurrence of deficiencies;
- show how the training of staff in new or revised operating methods is to be completed.

Where servicing is a specified requirement, suppliers should state their intentions to assure conformance to applicable servicing requirements, such as:

- regulatory and legislative requirements;
- industry codes and practices;
- service level agreements;
- training of customer personnel;
- availability of initial and ongoing support during the agreed time-period;
- statistical techniques, where relevant.

Note: ISO 10005 (Quality Management – Guidelines for Quality Plans) provides useful guidance on how to produce Quality Plans as well as including helpful suggestions on how to maintain an organisation's quality activities.

3 THE HISTORY OF QUALITY STANDARDS

Quality used to be about making sure that the product was right and with an emphasis on the manufacturer being required to produce something that could be inspected against a specific dimension or criterion. The product was then considered acceptable, or had to be reworked to become acceptable, or had to be scrapped (which could be very expensive). When things went wrong it was usual to blame the craftsmen (e.g. welders, painters, typists, etc.)!

Figure 3.1 Old fashioned Quality Control!

In the 1920's, a Munitions Standard was developed by the UK Ordnance Board to guarantee that bullets used during World War I were good (and safe!) enough to be fired. This standard is now known as Def Stan 13–131 and is the benchmark to which all munitions are measured.

Quite a lot of people have said that today's ISO 9000 originated from the 1920s munitions standard. We tend to believe, however, that the actual 'start' of ISO 9000 was probably during the US Navy Polaris submarine programme in the late 1950's when Admiral Hymen G. Rickover – for

Figure 3.2 This is *not* a good check for Quality!

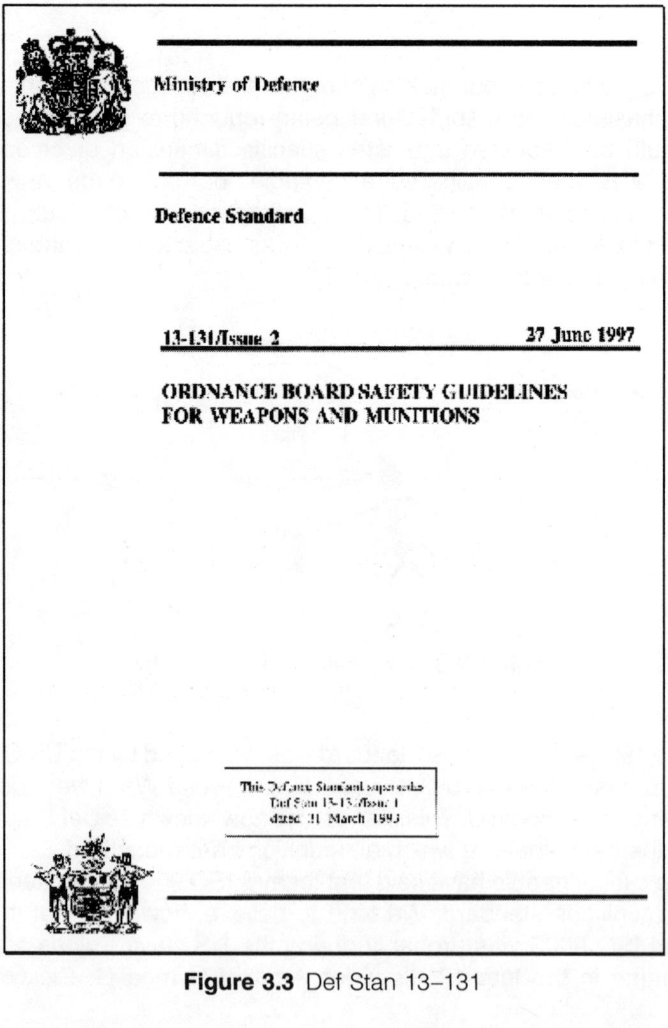

Ministry of Defence

Defence Standard

13-131/Issue 2   27 June 1997

ORDNANCE BOARD SAFETY GUIDELINES
FOR WEAPONS AND MUNITIONS

This Defence Standard supersedes
Def Stan 13-131/Issue 1
dated 31 March 1993

Figure 3.3 Def Stan 13–131

many years the head of the US Nuclear Navy, and renowned for having a ruthless disposition and a very hot temper – became frustrated at the delays caused by defects, errors and general quality breakdowns. He took thirty fresh graduates from Harvard, gave each of them a list of subcontractors to visit and investigate, a time scale and report format and then sent them out into the industrial jungle!

When they returned and the results were analysed, Rickover discovered that there were 18 major items which were the most common, or root cause of all the problems experienced. For example:

- **wrong materials obtained** – failure to specify totally and exactly what was required on the purchase orders;

Figure 3.4 Admiral Hymen G. Rickover – The founding father of Quality?

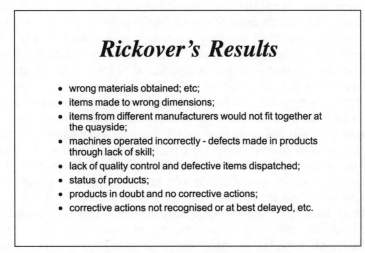

Rickover's Results

- wrong materials obtained; etc;
- items made to wrong dimensions;
- items from different manufacturers would not fit together at the quayside;
- machines operated incorrectly - defects made in products through lack of skill;
- lack of quality control and defective items dispatched;
- status of products;
- products in doubt and no corrective actions;
- corrective actions not recognised or at best delayed, etc.

Figure 3.5 Admiral Rickover's findings

- **items made to wrong dimensions** – failure to withdraw obsolete drawings when essential design changes had been made;
- **items from different manufacturers would not fit together at the quayside** – failure to calibrate measuring instruments to reliable reference standards which differed between organisations and districts;
- **machines operated incorrectly – defects made in products through lack of skill** – failure to train operators in performing vital tasks;
- **lack of quality control and defective items dispatched** – failure to inspect effectively;
- **status of products unknown** – no records available to show what had or had not been done;
- **products in doubt and no corrective actions taken** – no appointed person to ensure operations were conducted properly;
- **corrective actions not recognised or at best delayed, etc.** – top management were unaware of what was and was not happening.

The 18 points that emerged from the survey were then used as the cornerstone for quality in the American Space Research Programme (i.e. by NASA) and eventually became the basis of the first NATO AQAP specifications which defined the quality management system requirements to be adopted by all military subcontractors.

On a similar note, NASA's first major interplanetary project – the Ranger probe, designed to impact on the surface of the Moon – nearly failed, not just because of its advanced technology and the nature of this mission, but mainly due to a total lack of project management techniques.

JPL (Jet Propulsion Laboratory), who had become the main supplier of propulsion units after NASA was founded in 1958, drew upon its previous experience as a missile arsenal and resorted initially to a 'shoot and hope' testing philosophy. After five very expensive and awful failures, NASA, justifiably fed up with all the bad publicity, called a halt to the Ranger Project and convened a project review board to try to find out what was going wrong. NASA also recommended that JPL should **not** be awarded any major new projects until the Ranger problems had been sorted out – which was quite an incentive for JPL to find out what went wrong!

One of the main points that came out of the review was that the failure reporting system mainly relied on personal contact and there was no follow-up or formal supervision. The review also concluded that the project management should be enhanced with adequate staffing, clear lines of authority, formal design reviews, and strict quality control.

With all these changes in their quality system it was hardly surprising that on July 31 1964 NASA's spacecraft was launched as planned, and sent back high resolution images, right up until the point of impact with the lunar landscape.

3.1 1979

1979 was an important year for quality standards within the United Kingdom. The British Standards Institution (BSI) had already published a number of guides on quality assurance (e.g. BS 4891:1972 – A guide to Quality Assurance). With  the increased requirements for some sort of auditable quality assurance, BSI set up a study group to produce an acceptable document that would cover all requirements for a two party manufacturing or supply contract.

This became the BS 5750 series of standards on quality systems, which were first published in the United Kingdom during 1979. These standards supplied guidelines for internal quality management as well as external quality assurance. They were quickly accepted by manufacturers, suppliers and purchasers as being a reasonable minimum level of quality assurance that they could be expected to work to. The BS 5750 series thus became the 'cornerstone' for national quality.

American National Standards Institute

But in the meantime America had been working on their ANSI 90 series and other European countries were also busily developing their own sets of standards. Quite naturally, however, as the British Standards Institution had already produced and published an acceptable standard, most of these national standards were broadly based on BS 5750.

The concept was further developed by the defence, power generation, automobile and textile industries and gradually expanded from 18 initial points to 20 basic elements applicable to a very wide range of industries producing goods or services of many kinds.

3.2 1981

In 1981, the Department of Trade and Industry (DTI) formed a committee called 'FOCUS 'to examine areas where standardisation could benefit the competitive-  ness of British manufacturers and users of high technology – for instance Local Area Network (LAN) standardisation.

Owing to the wider international interest concerning quality assurance, the International Organisation for Standardisation (ISO) then set up a Study Group during 1983 to produce an international set of standards that all countries could use.

ORGANISATION
INTERNATIONALE DE
NORMALISATION

INTERNATIONAL
ORGANIZATION FOR
STANDARDIZATION

This initiative, Open Systems Interconnection (OSI), ensured those products from different manufacturers and different countries could exchange data and interwork in certain defined areas. In the United States, the Corporation of Open Systems (COS) was formed in 1986 to pursue similar objectives.

3.3 1987

Similar to quality standards from other countries, the ISO 9000 (1987) set of standards were very heavily based on BS 5750:1979 Parts 1, 2 and 3 and followed the same sectional layout except that an additional section (ISO 9000:1987 Part 0 Section 0.1) was introduced to provide further guidance about the principal concepts and applications contained in the ISO 9000 series.

When ISO 9000 was first published in 1987 it was immediately ratified by the United Kingdom (under the direction of the Quality Management and Statistics Standards Committee) and republished by the British Standards Institution (without deviation), as the new BS 5750 (1987) standard for Quality Management Systems.

Similarly, on 10 Dec. 1987 the Technical Board of the European Committee for Standardisation Commission [Europeen de Normalisation (CEN)] approved and accepted the text of ISO 9000:1987 as the European Standard – without modification – and republished it as EN 29000:1987.

At that time official versions of EN 29000 (1987) existed in English, French and German and other CEN members were allowed to translate any of these versions into their own language; they then had the same status as the original official versions.

Note: Up-to-date lists and bibliographical references concerning these and other European standards, may be obtained on application to the CEN Central Secretariat or from any CEN member (see Useful addresses at the end of this book).

BS 5750:1987 was, therefore, identical to ISO 9000:1987 and EN 29000:1987 except that BS 5750 had three additional guidance sections. Consequently, BS 5750 was not just the British Standard for 'Quality Management Systems' it was also **the** European and **the** international standard.

But, if all of these titles referred to the same quality standard, why not call the standard by the same name?!!

3.4 1994

Well that is exactly what happened. ISO, realising the problems of calling the same document by a variety of different names was confusing (even a bit ridiculous!), reproduced (in March 1994) the ISO 9000:1994 series of documents.

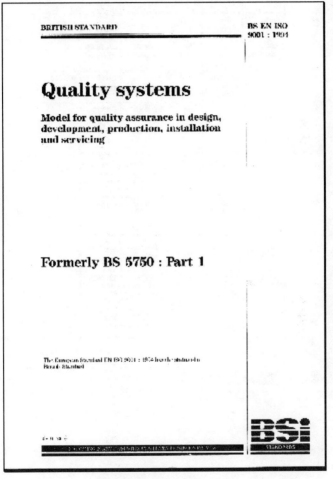

Figure 3.6 ISO 9001:1994

By the end of 1999 more than 60 countries had ratified ISO 9000 as their accepted quality standard and Table 3.1 shows some of the national standards that are equivalent to the ISO 9000 series.

Although the most notable change between the 1987 and the 1994 versions of the ISO 9000 standard was the streamlining of the numbering

Table 3.1 Comparison chart of equivalent standards to ISO 9000

Standard No	Equivalent Standard								
	AS	ASQC	BS	CSA	DIN	EN	IEC	JIS	NFX
ISO 9000	AS 3900	ASQC Q90		CSA Q9000	DIN ISO 9000	EN 29000		JIS-Z9900	NFX 50-121
ISO 9000/1		ASQC Q9000-1	BS EN ISO 9000 -1		DIN EN ISO 9000 PT1	EN ISO 9000/1			NFX 50-121
ISO 9000/2	AS 3900.2	ASQC Q9000-2							
ISO 9000/3		ASQC Q9000-3	BS 5750 PT13 (1991)	CSA Q9000.3	DIN ISO 9000 PT3	EN 29000 PT3			NFX 50-121/3
ISO 9000/4	AS 3900.4		BS 5750 PT14 (1993)		DIN ISO 9000 PT4	EN 60300 PT1	IEC 300 PT1		
ISO 9001	AS 3901	ASQC Q9001	BS EN ISO 9001	CSA Q9001	DIN EN ISO 9001 / DIN ISO 9001	EN ISO 9001		JIS-Z9901	NFX 50-131
ISO 9002	AS 3902	ASQC Q9002	BS EN ISO 9002	CSA Q9002	DIN EN ISO 9002 / DIN ISO 9002	EN ISO 9002		JIS-Z9902	NFX 50-132
ISO 9003	AS 3903	ASQC Q9003	BS EN ISO 9003	CSA Q9003	DIN EN ISO 9003 / DIN ISO 9003	EN ISO 9003		JIS-Z9903	NFX 50-133
ISO 9004	AS 3904	ASQC Q9004-1		CSA Q9004	DIN ISO 9004	EN 29004		JIS-Z9904	
ISO 9004/1		ASQC Q9004-1	BS EN ISO 9004-1		DIN EN ISO 9004 PT1	EN ISO 9004/1			
ISO 9004/2	AS 3904.2	ASQC Q9004-2	BS 5750 PT8 (1991)	CSA Q9004.2	DIN ISO 9004 PT2	EN 29004 PT2			NFX 50-122-2
ISO 9004/3	AS 3904.3	ASQC Q9004-3							
ISO 9004/4	AS 3904.4	ASQC Q9004-4	BS 7850 PT2 (1994)						

system, there were also around 250 other changes, the main ones being that:

- it became an explicit requirement that all members of an organisation (down to supervisory level at least) must have job profiles (descriptions) to define their authority and responsibility;
- design reviews became compulsory throughout the Work Package lifetime;
- documentation control was extended to ensure that all data was up to date.

Most of these 250 changes were intended to clarify the standard, making it easier to read. They did not significantly alter the way in which most organisations were running their businesses, merely seeking to improve it.

3.5 2000

With the end of the millennium there was no slowing down in the development of quality standards. As more and more organisations were expected to have ISO 9000 certification it became apparent that the existing structure of the standard would not suit all eventualities. This was especially relevant to the smaller organisations who did not necessarily have the resources to implement all the requirements.

With this in mind the members of ISO set about seeking the views of their members to see how the current standard could be improved. The result was the development of ISO 9001:2000.

ISO 9001:2000 is a significant refinement to ISO 9000:1994 and a more detailed explanation of its content and differences can be found in Chapter 5.

It is clear that there will be no let up in the quest for the ideal quality standard!

4 WHO PRODUCES QUALITY STANDARDS?

With literally thousands of standards available, on every conceivable topic, it can be difficult to decide which is important to you.

It has to be said, however, that standards are as international as the markets they serve and currently the main producers of national standards in Western Europe are:

- United Kingdom – British Standards Institution (BSI);
- Germany – Deutsch Institut fur Normung e.v. (DIN);
- France – Association Français de Normalisation (AFNOR).

Whilst the above countries are the primary source of European standards, there are others, as shown in Figure 4.2.

Outside Europe the most widely used standards come from:

- America – American National Standards Institute (ANSI);
- Canada – Canadian Standards Association (CSA).

There are others, of course (like Japan and Saudi Arabia), but these are the main two.

Although these countries publish what are probably the most important series of standards, virtually every country with an industrial base has its own national organisation producing its own national set of standards.

This diversity of standards can obviously lead to a lot of confusion, especially with regard to international trade and tenders. For example, if America were to invite tenders for a project quoting American (ANSI) National Standards as the minimum criteria, a European organisation could find it difficult to submit a proposal, either because it didn't have a copy of the relevant standard, or they wouldn't find it cost effective to retool their entire works in order to conform to the requirements of that particular American domestic standard.

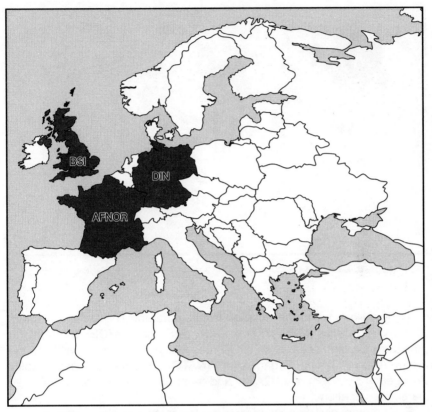

Figure 4.1 Main producers of national standards – Europe

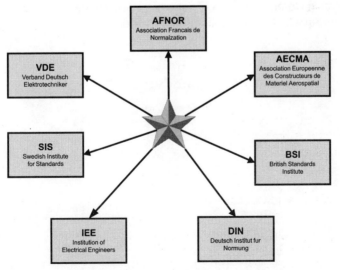

Figure 4.2 National and European standards

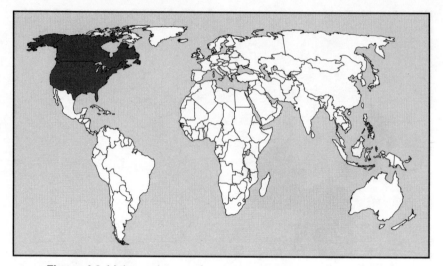

Figure 4.3 Main producers of national standards – outside Europe

In the military world the situation is little different. The United Kingdom Ministry of Defence (MOD-UK) use Defence Standards (DEF STANS), the American Division of Defense (DOD) use Military Standards (Mil-Std), the North Atlantic Treaty Organisation (NATO) use NATO Allied Quality Assurance Publications (AQAPs) and most other nations have their own particular variations.

From a more civilian point of view the International Telecommunications Union (ITU) Committees [i.e. The International Telegraph and Telephony Consultative Committee (CCITT) and the International Radio Consultative Committee (CCIR)] also publish recommendations.

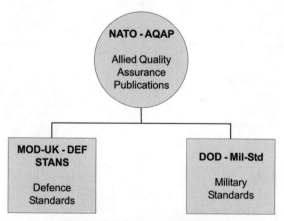

Figure 4.4 Military standards

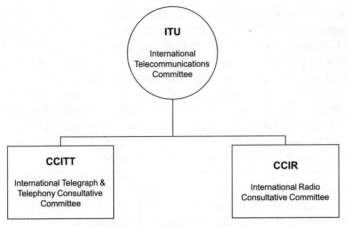

Figure 4.5 Civilian standards

Due to the diversity of publishers and publications within each country there has, therefore, been a steady growth in international standardisation and ISO and the IEC (International Electrotechnical Commission), are now the standards bodies that most countries are affiliated to – via, that is, their own particular National Standards Organisation (NSO).

Figure 4.6 International standards

ISO which was established as a United Nations Agency in 1947 is made up of representatives from more than 90 countries and includes BSI for the United Kingdom and ANSI for the United States. The work of ISO has increased considerably since it first got underway and a great number of standards are now available and have already been adopted.

These ISO and IEC standards (ISO is mainly concerned with industrial standards whilst IEC refers to electrical equipment) were initially published as 'recommendations', but they are now accepted as international standards in their own right and the use of the word 'shall' (i.e. denoting a mandatory requirement) is becoming commonplace.

The international standards are, themselves, drawn up by International Technical Committees which have been approved by ISO or IEC member countries and there are now many hundreds of different ISO and IEC Standards available, covering virtually every situation.

However, national bodies and national standards cannot dictate customer choice. A product that may legally be marketed need not be of universal appeal or internationally acceptable (for example, the three pin electrical plug used in the UK is totally useless in other countries!). Indeed, where different national standards persist they will do so as a reflection of different market preferences and national idiosyncrasies. For industry to survive in this new, 'liberalised' market, therefore, it must have a sound technological base supported by a comprehensive set of internationally approved standards.

'Quality' has thus become the key word in today's competitive markets and there are now more than 80 countries with similar organisations – most of which are members of ISO and IEC. Figure 4.7 shows the inter-relationship of these standards and committees.

From the consumer's point of view, the importance of international (i.e. ISO and IEC) standardisation is that all major agencies are now committed to recognising these standards. Equipment, modules and components can thus be designed and built so that they will be acceptable to all member countries. In this way interoperability is assured. (Perhaps, one day we may even see a European standard electrical plug!)

Thus today, there is a constant demand for new, revised and updated standards – particularly those with an international relevance. These standards could be for a product, a detailed material technical specification, broad guidelines, code of practice or for standards-based management systems. ISO 9000 (as the most successful and widely used series of Quality Management standards ever devised) have now become the benchmark for improving business efficiency and competitiveness.

It must not be forgotten, however, that the overall aim of standardisation is not just to produce paperwork that becomes part of a library. The aim is to produce a precise, succinct, readily applied and widely recognised set of principles, which are relevant and satisfy the varied needs of business, industry or commerce.

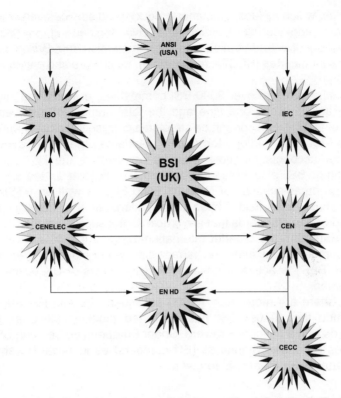

Figure 4.7 Inter-relationship of the various International Standards Bodies and Committees

The aim is also that standardisation shouldn't provide exclusive advantage to the products or services of one particular individual supplier and that the application of standards should always be capable of being verified by an independent third party evaluator (i.e. an auditor).

In the UK, the actual production of standards is set out in BS 0:1997 with its detailed:

- Guide to general principles of standardisation (Part 1);
- Guide to BSI committee procedures (Part 2);
- Guide to drafting and presentation of British Standards (Part 3).

Whilst the BSI advise that a proposal for a new standard can be made by anybody, they emphasise that the acceptance of the project by BSI has to depend on the support it can attract and, critically, the ability of the proposer – or anyone else who is able and willing – to provide an initial draft within a workable deadline. Work on new British Standards is authorised by BSI's Sector Committees. They decide the broad programme and priorities in their fields, which include consumer products and services, materials and chemicals, engineering, building and civil engineering, management systems, the electro-technical industry (for which the British Electro-Technical Committee (BEC) is responsible), healthcare and environmental concerns.

Currently there are over 3000 BSI committees, of which roughly 1000 may be active at any one time and the total number of members is in excess of 20,000. BSI committee structures correspond closely with those of other European and/or international standards organisations and their work now accounts for more than 90 per cent of the BSI standards programme. BSI also presents the British viewpoint to the European standards organisations, CEN and CENELEC, as well as ETSI in the telecommunications field. These organisations seek to develop harmonised European standards that are crucial to the success of the European Single Market. In the broader international arena, it is ISO and the IEC which pursue similar aims for harmonising world standards. Again BSI (with the BEC) is active in ensuring that the views of UK business are represented.

In all, there are more than 13,000 published ISO and IEC standards and, since the 1970s, BSI has published most of these as British Standards with a national foreword. Under European agreement, BSI also publishes European Standards (EN numbers) as identical British Standards, again with a national foreword.

5 WHAT IS ISO 9000:2000?

5.1 Background to the ISO 9001:2000 standard

When ISO 9000 was first released in 1987, it was recognised as being largely incomplete and required the auditors to fill in lots of the gaps. The first revision of ISO 9000 in 1994 got rid of many of these problems. However, an organisation could still conform to the standard but at the same time produce substandard products that were of a consistent poor quality! There was clearly a major loophole that enabled organisations to comply with the requirements of ISO 9000:1994 but without having to **improve** their quality!

Some managers also found it extremely difficult to see the real benefit of having to commit more and more manpower and finance to maintaining

Figure 5.1 The background to ISO 9001:2000

their ISO 9000 certification. Whilst most organisations accepted that the initial certification process was worthwhile and can result in some very real benefits, these are mainly one-offs. Once ISO 9000 had been fully adopted within an organisation, it was often felt that these savings could not be repeated. The ISO 9000 accreditation certificate has been hanging on the wall in the reception office for many years but third party surveillance visits don't tell them much more than they already knew from their own internal audits.

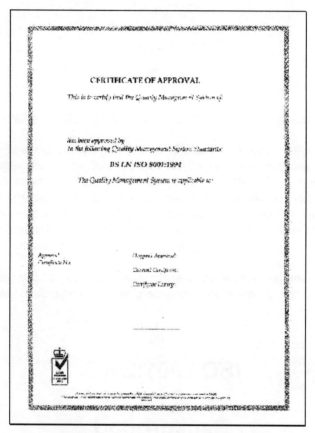

Figure 5.2 A typical ISO 9000 certificate

Quite a few organisations also felt that they had gone beyond ISO 9000 and apart from associating the organisation with a quality standard, there was little or no actual benefit to be gained from having to continually pay out for re-certification and surveillance fees.

According to the BSI, however, they frequently come across organisations who initially sought ISO 9000 registration (because it was a

Figure 5.3 The ever-increasing demand for ISO 9000 certification

requirement to continue business with a client), but having seen the benefits they, in turn, have pushed it on down their supply chain, thus increasing the requirement for ISO 9000 certification.

So as the 1990s progressed, more and more organisations started reaping benefits from the existing ISO 9000:1994 requirements but in turn also identified limitations within the series of standards. For example:

- some organisations did not need to carry out all of the 20 elements making up ISO 9000:1994 in order to be a quality organisation;
- the standard was too biased towards manufacturing industries and made it difficult for service industries to use;
- ISO 9000:1994 requirements were repeated in other management systems, resulting in duplication of effort (e.g. ISO 14001:1998 environmental management and BS 8800:1996 for the management of health and safety);
- many organisations wanted to progress beyond the confines of ISO 9000 towards Total Quality Management (TQM);
- the language used was not clear and could easily be misinterpreted;
- the standard was very inflexible and could not be tailored to specific industries, etc;
- the standard did not cater for continual improvement.

The reasons went on and on and there was clearly a need for revision.

Under existing international agreement, all International standards have to be re-inspected, 5 years after publication, for their continued applicability. In accordance with this agreement, ISO contacted more than 1,000 users and organisations for their views on ISO 9000:1994 using a questionnaire covering:

- problems with the existing standards;
- requirements for new/revised standards;

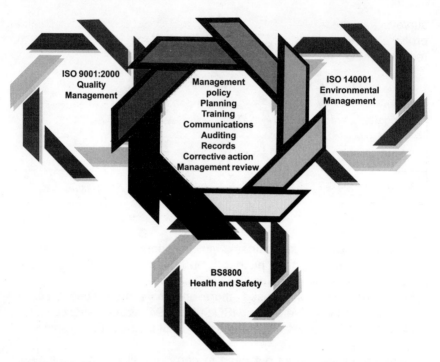

Figure 5.4 The common elements from ISO 9000, BS 8800 and ISO 14000

- possible harmonisation and interoperability between quality management, environmental management and health & safety standards.

The primary objective of this exercise was to make ISO 9001:2000:

- more compatible with other the management systems;
- more closely associated to business processes;
- more easily understood;
- capable of being used by all organisations, no matter their size;
- capable of used by all types of industries and professions (i.e. manufacturers **and** service providers);
- a means of continually improving quality;
- future proof.

5.2 The revision process

The revision process was the responsibility of ISO/TC176 (ISO Technical Committee No 176 'Quality Management and Quality Assurance'). Initial specifications and goals were established following extensive user surveys and these were followed by a user verification and validation process, to ensure that the standards produced would actually meet the requirements of the user.

The programme of work was as follows:

4th quarter 1997	1st Working Draft (WD1) for use by TC-176
1st quarter 1998	2nd Working Draft (WD2) for use by TC-176
2nd quarter 1998	3rd Working Draft (WD3) for use by TC-176
July 1998	Committee Draft (CD1) issued for ballot
February 1999	Committee Draft (CD2) issued for ballot
November 1999	Draft International Standard (DIS) for comment and vote by Member Countries*
September 2000	Publication of Final Draft International Standard (FDIS)
4th quarter 2000	Publication of International Standard (ISO)

*Once Draft International Standards have been adopted by the technical committees they are then circulated to member bodies for voting. Publication as an International Standard then requires a two-thirds majority of the votes.

5.2.1   Factors considered during the revision of the standards

Some of the factors considered during the development of the draft standards included:

- problems found with ISO 9001:1994's 20 element model and its bias towards manufacturing organisations;
- the increased use of the ISO 9000 standards by regulated industries (e.g. telecommunication, aircraft and automotive industries) and the subsequent need for change;
- the proliferation of guideline standards in the current ISO 9000 family (most of which were not fully used!);
- changed user requirements with more emphasis now being on meeting customer requirements;
- the difficulties that small businesses were having in trying to meet the requirements of the standards;

- the need to be more compatible with other management system standards such as ISO 14001 for environmental management;
- incorporation of the ISO 9000 standards into specific sector requirement standards or documents;
- the adoption of process-oriented management systems and the need to assist organisations in improving their business performance.

Figure 5.5 The ISO/TC 176 survey of ISO 9000:1994

The interest shown by users in improving ISO 9000:1994 was immediately obvious by their response to the questionnaires which resulted in over 6000 comments on each of the first and second committee drafts. The results of the survey clearly showed the need for a revised ISO 9000 standard, which would:

- be split, so that one standard (i.e. ISO 9001:2000) would address requirements, whilst another (ISO 9004:2000) would address the gradual improvement of an organisation's overall quality performance;
- be simple to use, easy to understand;
- only use clear language and terminology (a definite plus for most readers of current standards!);
- have a common structure based on a 'process model';
- be capable of being 'tailored' to fit all product and service sectors and all sizes of organisations (and not just the manufacturing industry);
- be capable of demonstrating continuous improvement and prevention of non-conformity;
- provide a natural stepping stone towards performance improvement;
- be more orientated toward continual improvement and customer satisfaction;
- have an increased compatibility with other management system standards (e.g. 14001);

- provide a basis for addressing the primary needs and interests of organisations in specific sectors such as aerospace, automotive, medical devices, telecommunications, and others.

The survey also showed that some organisations were finding it increasingly difficult to do business in the world marketplace without being ISO 9000 certified. Organisations, therefore, needed this recognition, but felt that gaining the ISO 9000 certification had been too difficult. The growing confusion about having three quality standards available for certification (i.e. ISO 9001:1994, 9002:1994 and 9003:1994) was also a problem and it was felt that the requirements of these three standards should be included into one overall standard (ISO 9001:2000).

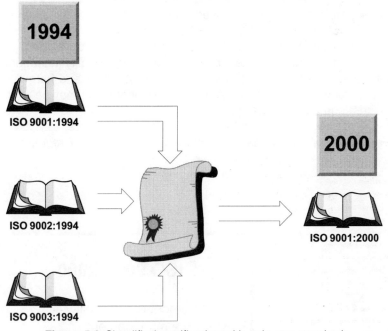

Figure 5.6 Simplified certification with only one standard

ISO emphasise, however, that the year 2000 revision of this ISO 9000 standards **should not** require the rewriting of an organisation's current Quality Management System (QMS) documentation! They point out that the major change was from a 'system based' to a more 'process based' management approach, which can be easily addressed by organisations who already have a fully documented QMS that complies with the 1994 standard.

5.2.2   Key changes in the standards

The main difference that you will find when reading ISO 9001:2000 is that the 20 elements contained in Section 4 of ISO 9001:1994 have now been replaced by four sections covering the management of resources, the quality of the product, the maintenance of quality records and the requirements for continual improvement.

- Each of the three main standards (i.e. ISO 9000:2000, ISO 9001:2000 and ISO 9004:2000) now have a revised title, which no longer includes the term *'quality assurance'*. This has been done in order to reflect the fact that the QMS requirements specified in these standards address quality assurance of product as well as customer satisfaction.
- ISO 9000:2000 now includes a description of the basic approach to quality management as well as including a revised vocabulary to reflect the usage of new and revised terms and associated definitions contained in ISO 9001:2000 and ISO 9004:2000.
- ISO 9001:2000 and ISO 9004:2000 have been developed as a *'consistent pair'* of QMS standards, based on eight quality management principles with a common process-oriented structure and harmonised terminology. They are designed to be used together, or may be used as stand-alone documents.
- ISO 9001:2000 is focused towards *'providing confidence, as a result of demonstration, in product conformance to established requirements'*

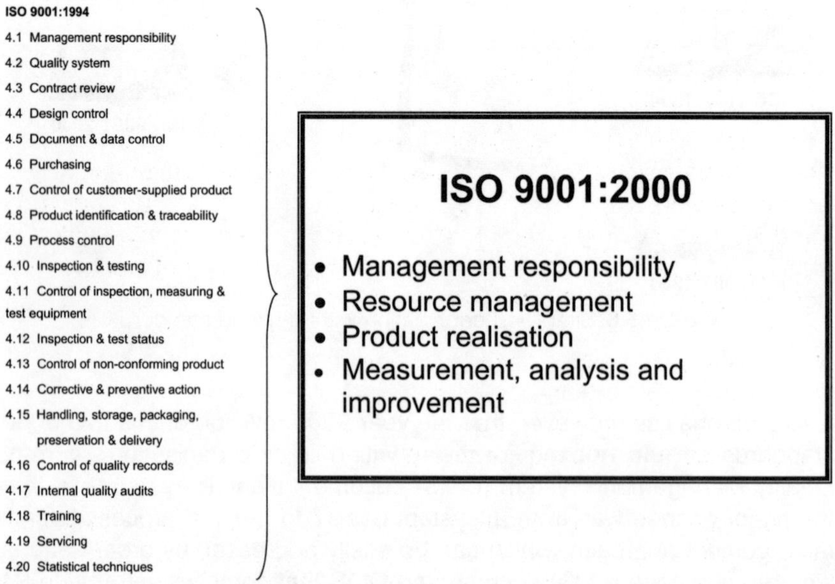

ISO 9001:1994

4.1 Management responsibility
4.2 Quality system
4.3 Contract review
4.4 Design control
4.5 Document & data control
4.6 Purchasing
4.7 Control of customer-supplied product
4.8 Product identification & traceability
4.9 Process control
4.10 Inspection & testing
4.11 Control of inspection, measuring & test equipment
4.12 Inspection & test status
4.13 Control of non-conforming product
4.14 Corrective & preventive action
4.15 Handling, storage, packaging, preservation & delivery
4.16 Control of quality records
4.17 Internal quality audits
4.18 Training
4.19 Servicing
4.20 Statistical techniques

ISO 9001:2000

- Management responsibility
- Resource management
- Product realisation
- Measurement, analysis and improvement

Figure 5.7 How 20 went into 4!

and includes a section entitled *'permissible exclusions'*. This section allows organisations to formally 'exclude' certain non-applicable requirements of the standard, yet still claim conformance to it. However, only those organisations that can **prove** that the nature of their products, customers and/or the applicable regulatory requirements do not need to meet the full requirements of ISO 9001:2000, are allowed these exclusions. For example, organisations whose products require no design activities (and who would have previously sought ISO 9002:1994 certification) can now claim to be in compliance with ISO 9001:2000 by excluding the requirements for design and/or development.

- ISO 9004:2000 is focused towards providing *'benefits for all interested parties through sustained customer satisfaction'*. ISO 9004:2000 also includes the requirements of ISO 9001:2000 in text boxes inserted in appropriate places (which means, perhaps, that organisations only need to purchase ISO 9004:2000 and not both of the standards – funny old world!).

- ISO 9004:2000 now includes an annex giving guidance on *'self-assessment'* to enable an organisation to check the status of their QMS. This will prove very useful for organisations who are considering applying for ISO 9001:2000 certification, but are unsure what additional quality documentation will be required.

Note: Small businesses wanting to work 'in conformance with ISO 9001:2000' are recommended to read *ISO 9001:2000 for Small Businesses* which is another of Ray Tricker's books in Butterworth-Heinemann's ISO 9000:2000 series.

One specific change to ISO 9001:2000 and ISO 9004:2000 that was brought about late in the day concerned the usage of the term 'product'. During the Committee Draft stages, it became apparent that there was a need to have a single word that described an organisation's output as well as the service that it provided. Consequently in the new standards, 'product' has been defined as *'the result of a set of interrelated or interacting activities which transform inputs into outputs'* and there are four agreed generic product categories, namely:

- hardware (e.g. engine mechanical part);
- software (e.g. computer program);
- services (e.g. transport);
- processed materials (e.g lubricant).

In practice, most products will, of course, be combinations of these four generic product categories. Whether the combined product is then called hardware, processed material, software or service will depend on the dominant element.

Figure 5.8 ISO 9001:2000 for Small Businesses

Although upgrading an organisation's QMS to ISO 9001:2000 will be fairly simple if that organisation is already certified to ISO 9001:1994, the impact on organisations who are currently only registered to ISO 9002:1994 and 9003:1994 (i.e. organisations not involved in the design and manufacture of a product) will probably be more difficult!

5.2.3 Accreditation, certification and registration

But what about certification and registration to this new standard?

Following consultation between ISO/TC 176, the International Accreditation Forum (IAF) and ISO/Committee of Conformity Assessment

Figure 5.9 The four generic product categories

(CASCO), a joint communiqué has been issued which includes the following statements:

- *'Accredited certificates to the new ISO 9001 shall not be granted until the publication of ISO 9001:2000 as an International Standard'.*
- *'Certification/registration body assessments to the latest draft of the new standard may begin prior to the publication of the ISO 9001:2000 International Standard'.*
- *'ISO 9001:2000 will require auditors and other relevant certification/ registration body personnel to demonstrate new competencies'.*
- *'Certification/registration bodies will need to take particular care in defining the scope of certificates issued to ISO 9001:2000, and the 'permissible exclusions' to the requirements of that standard'.*
- *'Certificates issued to ISO 9001:1994, ISO 9002:1994 or ISO 9003:1994 shall have a maximum validity of 3 years from the date of publication of ISO 9001:2000'.*

However, although organisations already registered to the 1994 standard will have up to 3 years following publication of the ISO 9001:2000 in which to re-certify, it is strongly recommended that, if you are one of these organisations, you make a start on the transition to the new standard as soon as possible. If your organisation was previously certified to ISO 9002:1994 or ISO 9003:1994 you will be allowed to work to this new international standard by reducing the scope of your conformance. For example, when a customer needs a particular type of product and/or service that does not necessarily require all the QMS requirements, then they can be excluded. This exclusion can be made, **provided** that you do not reduce the scope of your QMS or exclude any QMS requirements that affect your ability to provide a conforming product and/or service. All exclusions need to be defined in your Quality Manual and naturally, reducing the scope of conformance does not absolve you from providing a product and/or service which meets customer requirements.

As previously mentioned, the 2000 revision is also an attempt to harmonise the common quality management elements of ISO 9000 with those contained in the ISO 14000 series of environmental management system standards and, to some degree, the health and safety requirements of standards such as BS 8800. The overall intention is to enable an organisation to run one management system that addresses quality, the environment and health and safety.

It has to be said, however, that much of the old standard has been preserved and the revisions that have been made have been aimed mainly at closing the gap between ISO 9000, QS 9000 for the automotive industry and TR 9000 for the telecommunications industry etc.

5.3   The 'consistent pair'

In providing the new standards, ISO developed ISO 9001:2000 and ISO 9004:2000 with the same sequence and structure; so that it could form a 'consistent pair' of quality management standards which can be used either together or independently.

Whilst ISO 9001:2000 specifies the requirements for a QMS (that can be used by organisations for certification or contractual purposes), ISO 9004:2000 provides guidance aimed at improving an organisation's overall quality performance. ISO 9004:2000 is not, however, meant as a 'guideline for implementing ISO 9001:2000' nor is it intended for certification or contractual use.

Both of the standards are based on eight quality management principles, which reflect best management practices. These eight principles are:

- customer focus;
- leadership;
- involvement of people;
- process approach;
- system approach to management;
- continual improvement;
- factual approach to decision making;
- mutually beneficial supplier relationship.

Figure 5.10 The eight quality management principles

In summary ISO 9001:2000 now:

- is flexible enough to fit any sort organisation (i.e. the manufacturing emphasis is gone);
- no longer consists of 20 isolated elements;
- has a new quality process management model;
- defines responsibilities and authorities within the process areas;
- has a new emphasis on the identification of stakeholders and how the organisation plans to meet their needs;
- includes quality planning similar to the automotive industries advanced quality planning shown in QS 9000;
- sets a requirement for the regular review of quality objectives;
- provides a flexible approach to quality documentation;
- provides useful rules for presenting the Quality Manual;
- enables an organisation to assure that its infrastructure is sufficient to meet its quality objectives;
- provides a method for continually reviewing the work environment and its effect on quality;
- emphasises the identification and review of customer needs and expectations;
- needs a formal review of an organisation's ability to meet customer needs;
- emphasises close communications with customers;
- includes process capability studies;
- includes design control based on project management;
- includes expanded validation of design requirements;
- requires configuration management;
- gives a better definition of the function of purchasing and procurement;

- verifies purchased products;
- validates the output of processes within a organisation;
- replaces service requirements with delivery and post delivery service requirements;
- closely integrates with ISO 10012 'Quality Assurance Requirements for Measuring Equipment' concerning the use of measurement and inspection equipment;
- needs process measurements and process audits;
- documents how a product is measured and evaluated using a Quality (Control) Plan;
- includes the requirement for regular revalidation of products or services to ensure that they continue to meet customer expectations;
- requires a formal system of measuring customer satisfaction;
- gives a more aggressive definition of corrective and preventive action;
- requires a formal policy on continuous improvement;
- is in line with other management systems.

Thus all organisations, whether private or public, large or small, involved in the production of manufactured goods, services, or software, have tools available to organise their activities.

5.4   Compatibility with ISO 14001:1996

ISO 9001:2000 is intended to be compatible with other management system standards, in particular, those relating to environmental management, occupational health & safety and financial management. In producing ISO 9001:2000, TC176 have made sure that the requirements of ISO 14001:1996 'Environmental Management Systems – Specification with guidance for use' have been carefully considered and a very good degree of compatibility now exists between these two standards. Work is already underway to produce a revised edition of ISO 14001 (scheduled for 2002) with the aim of achieving even more compatibility.

Whilst ISO 9001:2000 does not, however, include any requirements that are specific to any of this, and indeed any other management system, it does, nevertheless, allow an organisation to align and integrate its own QMS with other (related) management system requirements. In some cases, it may even be possible for an organisation to adapt its existing management system(s) in order to establish a QMS that complies with the requirements of ISO 9001:2000.

5.5   The ISO 9000:2000 family of standards

The ISO 9000:2000 family of standards consists of three primary standards supported by a number of technical reports. These are:

1 **ISO 9000:2000 Quality Management Systems – Fundamentals and vocabulary** (superseding ISO 8402:1994 'Quality Management and Quality Assurance – Vocabulary' and ISO 9000–1:1994 'Quality Management and Quality Assurance Standards – Guidelines for selection and use').

   Describes fundamentals of QMSs which forms the subject of the ISO 9000 family, and defines related terms.

2 **ISO 9001:2000 Quality Management Systems – Requirements** (superseding ISO 9001:1994 ' Quality Systems – Model for quality assurance in design, development, production, installation and servicing', ISO 9002:1994 'Quality Systems – Model for quality assurance in production, installation and servicing' and ISO 9003:1994 'Quality Systems – Model for quality assurance in final inspection and test').

   Specifies the requirements for QMSs for use where an organisation's capability to provide products that meet customer and applicable regulatory requirements needs to be demonstrated.

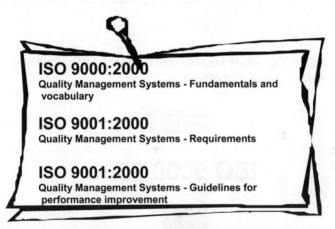

Figure 5.11 The ISO 9000:2000 family

3 **ISO 9004:2000 Quality Management Systems – Guidelines for performance improvement** (superseding ISO 9004–1:1994 'Quality Management and Quality System Elements – Guidelines).

   Provides guidance on QMSs, including the processes for continual improvement that will contribute to the satisfaction of an organisation's customers and other interested parties.

For completeness, a new standard is being written to assist auditing systems against ISO 9001:2000, this will be:

ISO 19011 Guidelines on auditing quality and environmental management systems (to supersede ISO 10011–1:1990 ' Guidelines for Auditing Quality Systems – Auditing', ISO 1011–2:1991 'Guidelines for Auditing Quality Systems – Qualification criteria for quality system auditors', ISO 1011–3:1991 'Guidelines for Auditing Quality Systems – Management of audit programmes', as well as ISO 14010:1996 'Guidelines for Environmental Auditing – General principles', ISO 14011:1996 'Guidelines for Environmental Auditing – Audit procedures – Auditing of environmental management systems' and ISO 14012:1996 'Guidelines for Environmental Auditing – Qualification criteria for environmental auditors').

This new standard will provide guidance on managing and conducting environmental and quality audits. Currently this standard is at the Committee Draft stage, but it is scheduled for publication during the third quarter 2001.

Note: All of the other standards and documents within the ISO 9000:1994 family that were submitted for formal review by ISO member bodies during the committee stages will probably be withdrawn in the near future.

5.5.1   ISO 9000:2000 Quality Management Systems – Fundamentals and vocabulary

Figure 5.12 The way to ISO 9000:2000

To ensure a more harmonised approach to standardisation (and the hopeful(!) achievement of coherent terminology within the ISO 9000:2000 family), the development of ISO 9000:2000 was completed in parallel with ISO 9001:2000, ISO 9004:2000, the future ISO 14001 standard for environmental management and all other existing and planned management standards.

ISO 9001:2000 includes a revision of the current ISO 8402:1994 'Quality Management and Quality Assurance – Vocabulary' standard, provides a more formal approach to the definition of terms, specifies terminology for QMSs and will assist:

- those concerned with enhancing the mutual understanding of the terminology used in quality management (e.g. suppliers, customers, regulators);
- internal or external auditors, regulators, certification and/or registration bodies;
- developers of related standards.

ISO 9000:2000 also provides an introduction to the fundamentals of QMSs and following publication of this standard, ISO 8402:1994 and ISO 9000–1:1999 have been withdrawn.

5.5.2   ISO 9001:2000 Quality Management Systems – Requirements

Figure 5.13 The way to ISO 9001:2000

The current ISO 9001:1994, ISO 9002:1994 and ISO 9003:1994 standards have now been consolidated into a single revised ISO 9001:2000 standard. Organisations that have previously used ISO 9002:1994 and ISO 9003:1994 will be allowed to be certified to ISO 9001:2000 through a *'reduction in scope'* of the standard's requirements by omitting requirements that do not apply to their particular organisation.

With the publication of ISO 9001:2000, there is now, therefore, a single quality management **'requirements'** standard that is applicable to all organisations, products and services. It is the only standard that can be used for the certification of a QMS and its generic requirements can be used by **any** organisation to:

- address customer satisfaction;
- meet customer and applicable regulatory requirements;
- enable internal and external parties (including certification bodies) to assess the organisation's ability to meet these customer and regulatory requirements.

For certification purposes, your organisation will now have to possess a documented management system which takes the inputs and transforms them into targeted outputs. Something that effectively:

- says what they are going to do;
- does what they have said they are going to do;
- keep records of everything that they do – especially when things go wrong.

The basic process to achieve these targeted outputs will encompass:

- the client's requirements;
- the inputs from management and staff;
- documented controls for any activities that are needed to produce the finished article;
- and, of course, delivering a product or service which satisfies the customer's original requirements.

The adoption of a QMS has to be a strategic decision of any organisation and the design and implementation of their QMS will be

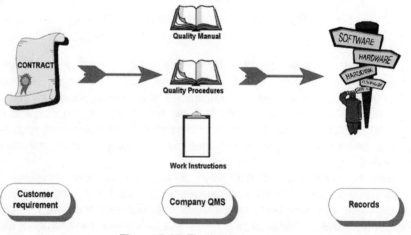

Figure 5.14 The basic process

influenced by its varying needs, objectives, products provided, processes employed and the size and structure of that organisation. As ISO are quick to point out, however, it is not the intention of ISO 9001:2000 to insist on a uniform structure to QMSs, or uniformity of documentation and the QMS requirements specified in this standard should always be viewed as complementary to product technical requirements.

The ISO 9001:2000 standard is the only standard within the 2000 edition to which an organisation can be certified. It includes all the key points from the previous 20 elements of ISO 9001:1994, but integrates them into four major generic business processes, namely:

- **Management responsibility** (policy, objectives, planning, system, review);
- **Resource management** (human resources, information, facilities)
- **Product realisation** (customer, design, purchasing, production, calibration);
- **Measurement, analysis and improvement** (audit, process/product control, improvement).

Figure 5.15 The four major generic business processes of ISO 9001:2000

The new structure of ISO 9001:2000 is as shown in Table 5.1.

We have included Table 5.2 showing the correlation between the existing key elements from ISO 9001:1994 and the sections of ISO 9001:2000 with the aim of assisting organisations wishing to change over their existing ISO 9000:1994 QMS to the 2000 edition.

Table 5.1 The structure of ISO 9001:2000

Section	Title
1	**Scope**
1.1	General
1.2	Application
2	**Normative reference**
3	**Terms and definitions**
4	**Quality Management System**
4.1	General requirements
4.2	Documentation requirements
4.2.1	General
4.2.2	Quality Manual
4.2.3	Control of documents
4.2.4	Control of quality records
5	**Management responsibility**
5.1	Management commitment
5.2	Customer focus
5.3	Quality policy
5.4	Planning
5.4.1	Quality objectives
5.4.2	Quality management system planning
5.5	Responsibility, authority and communication
5.5.1	Responsibility and authority
5.5.2	Management representative
5.5.3	Internal communication
5.6	Management review
5.6.1	General
5.6.2	Review input
5.6.3	Review output
6	**Resource management**
6.1	Provision of resources
6.2	Human resources
6.2.1	General
6.2.2	Competence, awareness and training
6.3	Infrastructure
6.4	Work environment

Table 5.1 *Continued*

Section	Title
7	**Product realisation**
7.1	Planning of product realisation
7.2	Customer-related processes
7.2.1	Determination of requirements related to the product
7.2.2	Review of requirements related to the product
7.2.3	Customer communication
7.3	Design and development
7.3.1	Design and development planning
7.3.2	Design and development inputs
7.3.3	Design and development outputs
7.3.4	Design and development review
7.3.5	Design and development verification
7.3.6	Design and development validation
7.3.7	Control of design and development changes
7.4	Purchasing
7.4.1	Purchasing process
7.4.2	Purchasing information
7.5	Production and service provision
7.5.1	Control of production and service provision
7.5.2	Validation of processes for production and service provision
7.5.3	Identification and traceability
7.5.4	Customer property
7.5.5	Preservation of product
7.6	Control of measuring and monitoring devices
8	**Measurement, analysis and improvement**
8.1	General
8.2	Monitoring and measurement
8.2.1	Customer satisfaction
8.2.2	Internal audit
8.2.3	Monitoring and measurement of processes
8.2.4	Monitoring and measurement of product
8.3	Control of non-conformity
8.4	Analysis of data
8.5	Improvement
8.5.1	Continual improvement
8.5.2	Corrective action
8.5.3	Preventive action

Table 5.2 Correlation between the clauses of ISO 9001:1994 and the sections of ISO 9001:2000

ISO 9001:1994	FDIS ISO 9001:2000
1. Scope	1
2. Normative reference	2
3. Definitions	3
4. Quality system requirements	
4.1 Management responsibility	
4.1.1 Quality policy	5.1, 5.3, 5.4.1
4.1.2 Organisation	
4.1.2.1 Responsibility & authority	5.5.1
4.1.2.2 Resources	5.1, 6.1, 6.2.1, 6.3
4.1.2.3 Management representative	5.5.2
4.1.3 Management review	5.6.1, 5.6.2, 5.6.3, 8.5.1
4.2 Quality system	
4.2.1 General	4.1, 4.2.1, 4.2.2, 5.1, 5.4.1
4.2.2 Quality system procedures	4.2.1
4.2.3 Quality planning	5.4.2, 6.2.1, 7.1
4.3 Contract review	5.2, 7.2.1, 7.2.2, 7.2.3
4.4 Design control	7.2.1, 7.3.1, 7.3.2, 7.3.3, 7.3.4, 7.3.5, 7.3.6, 7.3.7
4.5 Document & data control	4.2.1, 4.2.3
4.6 Purchasing	7.4.1, 7.4.2, 7.4.3, 7.4.4
4.7 Control of customer-supplied product	7.5.4
4.8 Product identification & traceability	7.5.3
4.9 Process control	6.3, 6.4, 7.1, 7.5.1, 7.5.2, 8.2.3
4.10 Inspection & testing	7.1, 7.4.3, 7.5.1, 7.5.3, 8.1, 8.2.4
4.11 Control of inspection, measuring and test equipment	7.6
4.12 Inspection & test status	7.5.3
4.13 Control of non-conforming product	8.3
4.14 Corrective & preventive action	8.4, 8.5.2, 8.5.3
4.15 Handling, storage, packaging, preservation & delivery	7.5.1, 7.5.5
4.16 Control of quality records	4.2.4
4.17 Internal quality audits	8.2.2, 8.2.3
4.18 Training	6.2.1, 6.2.2
4.19 Servicing	7.1, 7.5.1
4.20 Statistical techniques	8.1, 8.2.3, 8.2.4, 8.4

Notes
1. Reference numbers are given in numerical order, not in order of significance.
2. The clause numbers in ISO 9001:2000 are as follows:
    5.x.x. – Management Responsibility
    6.x.x. – Resource Management
    7.x.x. – Product Realisation
    8.x.x. – Measurement, Analysis and Improvement

5.6 Major changes caused by ISO 9001:2000

5.6.1 The process model

ISO 9001:2000 uses eight quality management principles which reflect best practice and which are designed to enable a continual improvement of the business, its overall efficiency and be capable of responding to customer needs and expectations.

The eight principles contained in ISO 9001:2000 are of primary concern to an organisation, as they will affect an organisation's overall approach to quality. They are:

1 **Customer focus:** Organisations depend on their customers and therefore should understand current and future customer needs should meet customer requirements and should strive to exceed customer expectations.
2 **Leadership:** Leaders establish unity of purpose, direction, and the internal environment of their organisation. They create the environment in which people can become fully involved in achieving the organisation's objectives.
3 **Involvement of people:** People at all levels are the essence of an organisation and their full involvement enables their abilities to be used for the organisation's benefit.
4 **Process approach:** A desired result is achieved more efficiently when related resources and activities are managed as a process.
5 **System approach to management:** Identifying, understanding and managing a system of inter-related processes for a given objective contributes to the effectiveness and efficiency of the organisation.
6 **Continual improvement:** Continual improvement is a permanent objective of any organisation.
7 **Factual approach to decision making:** Effective decisions are based on the logical and intuitive analysis of data and information.
8 **Mutually beneficial supplier relationships:** Mutually beneficial relationships between an organisation and its suppliers enhance the ability of both organisations to create value.

5.7 Brief summary of ISO 9001:2000 requirements

ISO 9001:2000 consists of eight sections which are summarised below. For a more complete description please see 'ISO 9001:2000 for Small Businesses' by Ray Tricker from Butterworth-Heinemann's 'ISO 9000:2000' series.

5.7.1   Section 1 – Scope

This is a short section explaining what the standard covers.

5.7.2   Section 2 – Normative reference

Another short section which contains details of other standards that form a mandatory input to ISO 9001:2000. In this instance the only reference is ISO 9000:2000 'Quality Management Systems – Fundamentals and vocabulary'.

5.7.3   Section 3 – Terms and definitions

The third section explains how the standard is based on a supply chain concept as shown in Figure 5.16.

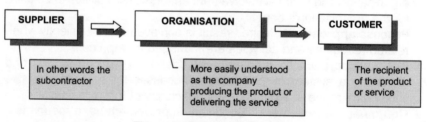

Figure 5.16 The supply chain

Note: The term 'supplier' was used previously in ISO 9000:1994. ISO 9000:2000 has replaced this with 'organisation'.

5.7.4   Section 4 – Quality Management System

This section makes it mandatory for an organisation to have a documented QMS that defines the processes necessary to ensure that the product conforms to customer requirements. This QMS must be implemented, maintained and, most importantly, continually improved by the organisation.

It should be noted that the extent of the QMS documentation (which may be in any form or type of medium) is dependent on the:

- size and type of the organisation;
- complexity and interaction of the processes;
- competency of personnel.

5.7.5   Section 5 – Management responsibility

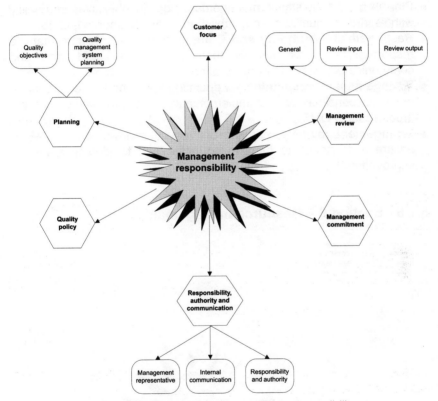

Figure 5.17 Section 5 – management responsibility

This section contains the majority of the old ISO 9001:1994 management responsibility and quality requirements all rolled together. It is broken down into the following sub-clauses that cover the requirements for:

- **Management commitment** – top (i.e. senior) management committing, fully, to the development and implementation of the QMS and continually improving its effectiveness. (Without their commitment the system will fall at the first hurdle);

- **Customer focus** – determining, fully understanding and documenting customer requirements; ensuring compliance with identified statutory legislation (e.g. EC Directives, other national and international standards etc);
- **Quality policy** – ensuring that the Quality Policy is appropriate for the purpose, includes a commitment to comply with requirements (and improve the effectiveness of the QMS), is understood by everyone and reviewed for continued suitability;
- **Planning** – clearly stating management's quality objectives and policy with regards to quality in an established, fully documented, QMS;
- **Responsibility, Authority and Communication** – ensuring that the responsibilities, authorities and their interrelations are defined (and communicated) within the organisation;
- **Management representative** – appointing someone (or some people) to be responsible for the implementation and improvement of the organisation's QMS;
- **Management review** – carrying out regular reviews of the QMS to ensure it continues to function correctly (and to identify areas for improvement).

5.7.6   Section 6 – Resource management

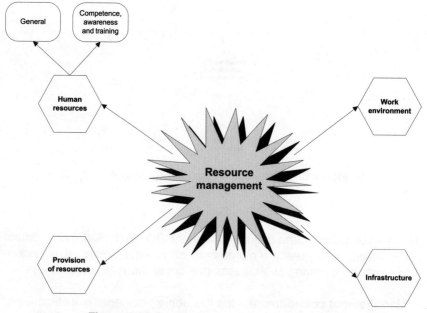

Figure 5.18 Section 6 – resource management

This section covers resources with regard to training, induction, responsibilities, working environment, equipment requirements, maintenance etc. It is broken down into the following sub-sections that cover the requirements for:

- **Provision of resources** – identifying the resources required to implement and improve the processes that make up the QMS;
- **Human resources** – assigning personnel with regard to competency, education, training, skill and/or experience;
- **Facilities** – identifying, providing and maintaining the workspace, facilities, equipment (hardware and software) and supporting services to achieve conformity of product;
- **Work environment** – identifying and managing the work environment (e.g. health and safety, ambient conditions etc.).

5.7.7 Section 7 – Product realisation

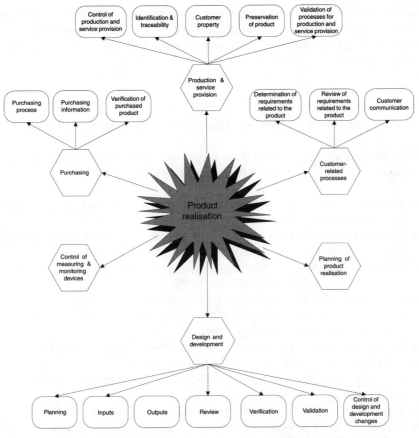

Figure 5.19 Section 7 – product realisation

This section absorbs most of the 20 elements of the old ISO 9000:1994 standard, including process control, purchasing, handling and storage, and measuring devices. This section is broken down into a number of sub-sections that cover the requirements for:

- **Planning product realisation** – clearly defining and documenting the processes used to ensure reliable and consistent products (e.g. verification and validation activities, criteria for acceptability and quality records etc.);
- **Customer-related processes** – identifying customer, product, legal and design requirements;
- **Design and development** – controlling the design process (e.g. design inputs, outputs, review, verification, validation and change control);
- **Purchasing** – having documented processes for the selection and control of suppliers and the control of purchases that affect the quality of the finished product or service;
- **Production and service provision** – having documented instructions that control the manufacture of a product or delivery of a service;
- **Control of measuring and monitoring devices** – their control, calibration and protection.

5.7.8   Section 8 – Measurement, analysis and improvement

This section absorbs the former inspection and measurement control sections of ISO 9001:1994. It includes requirements for:

- **Planning** – defining the requirements for measurement analysis and improvement (including statistical analysis);
- **Customer satisfaction** – monitoring customer satisfaction/dissatisfaction as a measurement and improvement of the QMS;
- **Internal audits** – conducting periodic internal audits to confirm continued conformity with ISO 9001:2000;
- **Measurement and monitoring of processes and product** – defining processes to monitor the performance of the QMS and the products and services delivered by the organisation;
- **Non-conformity** – controlling non-conformity and its rectification;
- **Data analysis** – collecting and analysing statistical data obtained from the organisation's measuring and monitoring activities to find areas of improvement;
- **Improvement** – planning for continual improvement of the QMS;
- **Corrective and preventive action** – having available procedures to address corrective and preventive action.

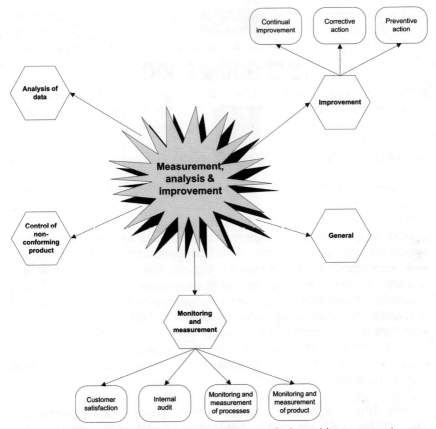

Figure 5.20 Section 8 – measurement, analysis and improvement

5.8   ISO 9004:2000 Quality Management Systems – Guidelines for performance improvement

ISO 9004:2000 provides guidance on QMSs, including the processes that are required for continual improvement and, ultimately, customer satisfaction. The guidance should be viewed as generic and with the overall aim of being applicable to all organisations, regardless of the type, size and the product provided. It is based on the provisions of the ISO 9004:1994 series.

ISO 9004:2000 is aimed at improving an organisation's overall quality performance and provides a stepping stone to Total Quality Management (TQM). In the words of the standard, *'ISO 9004:2000 is designed to go beyond quality management requirements and provide organisations with guidelines for performance improvement through sustained customer satisfaction. In doing so it:*

Figure 5.21 The reason for ISO 9004:2000

- *provides guidance to management on the application and use of a QMS to improve an organisation's overall performance;*
- *is recommended as a guide for organisations whose management wishes to move beyond the minimum requirements of ISO 9001 in pursuit of increased performance improvement ISO 9004 is not intended as guidance for compliance with ISO 9001;*
- *defines the minimum QMS requirements needed to achieve customer satisfaction by meeting specified product requirements;*
- *can be also be used by an organisation to demonstrate its capability to meet customer requirements'.*

Note: This international standard is not a guideline for implementing ISO 9001 and is not intended for certification, regulatory or contractual use.

6 HOW QUALITY HELPS DURING A PRODUCT'S LIFE CYCLE

In the previous chapters we learnt how to produce a correctly structured Quality Management System (QMS) and in Chapter 5 we saw the requirements that this QMS would have to meet. However, you may well still be saying, that is all well and good, but how will it help me improve quality in my organisation?

In this chapter we will look at all the areas that can be influenced by quality during the life of a product. This will clearly show even the most cynical of readers that there is no part of a business that cannot be improved by incorporating quality into your management system.

To start with you have to appreciate that there are a number of stages during a product's lifecycle where quality assurance has an influence.

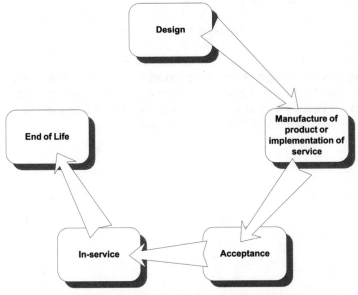

Figure 6.1 Quality Assurance lifecycle

6.1   Design stage

'Quality must be designed into a product before manufacture or assembly' (ISO 9004:2000).

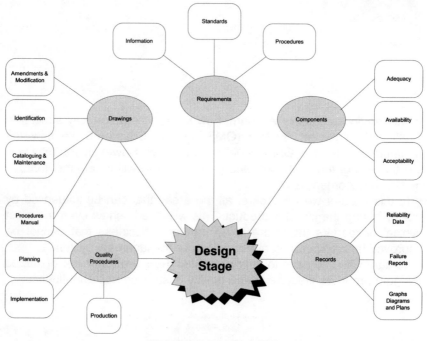

Figure 6.2 Design stage

Throughout the design stage of a product the quality of that design must be regularly checked. Quality Procedures (QPs) have to be planned, written and implemented so as to predict and evaluate the fundamental and intrinsic reliability of the proposed design.

6.2 Manufacturing stage

'Manufacturing operations must be carried out under controlled conditions' (ISO 9004:2000).

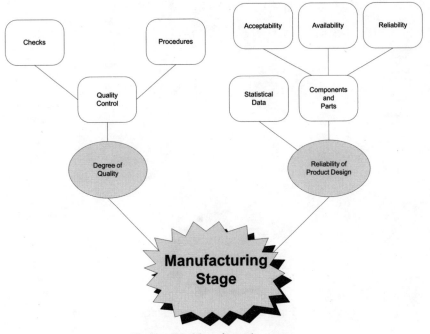

Figure 6.3 Manufacturing stage

During all manufacturing processes, (and throughout early in-service life), the product must be subjected to a variety of quality control procedures and checks in order to evaluate the degree of quality.

6.3 Acceptance stage

'The Quality of a product must be proved before being accepted'
(ISO 9004:2000).

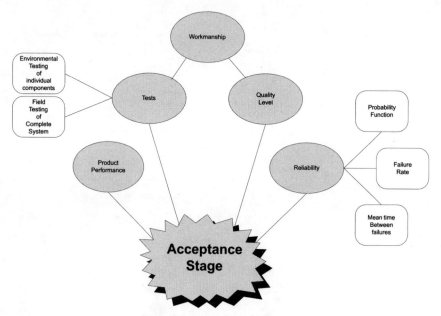

Figure 6.4 Acceptance stage

During the acceptance stage, the product is subjected to a series of tests designed to confirm that the workmanship of the product fully meets the levels of quality required (or stipulated) by the user and that the product performs the required function correctly. Tests will range from environmental tests of individual components to field testing complete products.

6.4 In-service stage

'Evaluation of product performance during typical operating conditions and feedback of information gained through field use – improves product capability' (ISO 9004:2000).

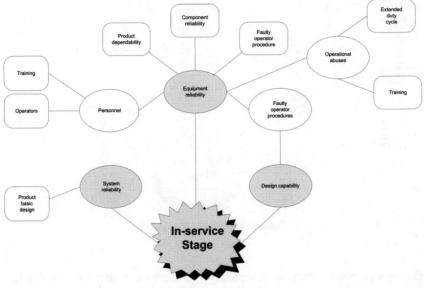

Figure 6.5 In-service stage

During the in-service stage the equipment user is, of course, principally concerned with product reliability.

6.5   End of life stage

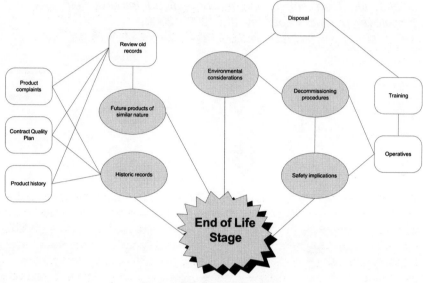

Figure 6.6 End of life stage

Designing, manufacturing, accepting and using a product is not the full story. Eventually that product will come to the end of its useful life either through age, fault or more than likely (because it has been built to such a high quality!) it has been overtaken by technology. Before throwing the redundant piece of equipment onto the rubbish heap, however, it is essential that a fully documented, historical record, of its design, use, problems, advantages and disadvantages etc. is assembled. This would normally be left up to the Quality Manager to organise.

So if you can incorporate quality into all five stages within the life of a product then you can have total control over your own success . . . or failure!

7 WHO CONTROLS QUALITY IN AN ORGANISATION?

Do not think for one minute that quality is the sole responsibility of the Quality Manager. You would even be wrong to think that the buck stops with senior management. Why not the staff? After all, they are responsible for physically incorporating quality into a product. Some may even foolishly say that the Quality Manual sitting on the shelf is the only control they need. The answer to who controls quality is very simple. **Everyone and everything** within an organisation has a part to play.

So what responsibilities do each of these groups of people have?

Who Controls Quality in a company?

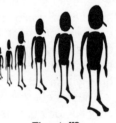

The Quality
Management
Team?

Management?

The staff?

Figure 7.1 Everyone has an impact on quality

7.1 Management

The main requirement of the organisation's management is that they establish, define and document their organisation's policy, objectives and commitments to quality.

As we have seen in the previous chapters, this documented system is usually presented as a Quality Manual. The Quality Manual must include details of the organisation's QMS and the aims, policies, organisation and procedures that are essential to demonstrate that they agree with the requirements of the relevant standard (e.g. ISO 9000 or ISO 14000).

Having established their overall position, the management will then have to:

- develop, control, co-ordinate, supervise and monitor their corporate quality policy and ensure that this policy is understood and maintained throughout the organisation;
- ensure that the organisation's QMS always meets the requirements of the national, European or international standard that the particular organisation has chosen to work to and where this fails to happen, see that corrective actions are carried out;
- define objectives such as fitness for use;
- ensure that the performance, safety and reliability of a product is correct and make sure that the costs associated with these objectives are kept to a reasonable figure.

7.2 Quality Management Team

As previously described, quality assurance is concerned with a consistency of quality and an agreed level of quality. To achieve these aims an organisation must be firmly committed to the fundamental principle of consistently supplying the right quality product. Equally, a purchaser must be committed to the fundamental principle of only accepting the right quality product.

Thus, a commitment within all levels of an organisation (manufacturer, supplier or purchaser) to the basic principles of quality assurance and quality control is required. It is, therefore, essential that a completely separate and independent division is formed to deal solely with quality matters. The organisation and duties of this section would usually look something like that shown in Figure 7.2.

For organisations who cannot justify the cost of employing full time inspectors, other options are available, such as:

- selecting personnel from existing staff who are not directly involved with a production process. They are then able to act as independent unbiased assessors;

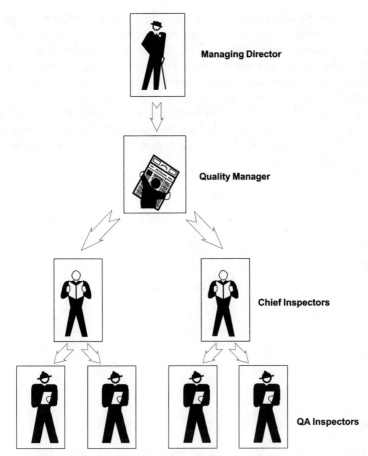

Figure 7.2 Quality management structure for a typical large organisation

- employing third party quality consultants, on a temporary basis, to carry out fully independent quality controls.

7.2.1 Quality Manager

The first requirement is for the organisation to nominate an individual who will be solely responsible to the management for the implementation and maintenance of the Quality Management System. This person is generally called the 'Quality Manager'.

The Quality Manager will answer directly to the Managing Director and will be responsible for all matters regarding the quality of the end product together with the activities of **all** sections within the organisation's premises.

Whilst there is a specific requirement within ISO 9001:2000 to appoint a member of staff to be directly responsible for quality management, this doesn't mean that you necessarily **have** to have a Quality Manager. In small organisations quality management might be part of the General Manager's duties. Regardless of who it may be, however, it is essential that this person is someone who is completely independent of any manufacturing or user function and has a thorough working knowledge of the requirements and recommendations of ISO 9001:2000.

In addition, owing to the importance of quality assurance, it is essential that the person selected for this position is fully qualified (both technically and administratively) and can quickly exert (show) his position and authority.

Managing Director

Quality Manager

Operation of the Quality Management System

| Design of Quality Manual |
| Design of Quality Plan |
| Preparation and Maintenance of Procedures |
| Quality Records |
| Quality Audits |
| Change Control |

Figure 7.3 Responsibilities of the Quality Manager

The Quality Manager's job is usually a very busy one, even in a small organisation(!) and the Quality Manager's responsibilities are spread over a wide area which covers all of the organisation's operations, as shown below.

7.2.1.1 General functional description

The Quality Manager is responsible for ensuring that the organisation's QMS is defined, implemented, audited and monitored in order to ensure that the organisation's deliverables comply with both the customer's quality and safety requirements together with the requirements of ISO 9001:2000.

7.2.1.2 Tasks

The Quality Manager normally reports directly to the Managing Director. His tasks shall include:

- ensuring the consistency of the organisation's QMS;
- ensuring compliance of the organisation's QMS with ISO 9001:2000;
- maintenance and effectiveness of the organisation's QMS;
- ensuring that the quality message is transmitted to and understood by everyone.

7.2.1.3 Responsibilities

The Quality Manager is responsible for:

- ensuring that the Quality Manual and individual Quality Plans are kept up to date;
- assisting and advising with the preparation of organisation's procedures;
- producing, reviewing and updating the organisation's QMS;
- ensuring compliance with the organisation's QMS by means of frequent audits;
- maintaining organisation quality records;
- producing, auditing and maintaining project Quality Plans;
- identifying potential/current problem areas within the organisation's life cycle through analysis of organisation statistics;
- holding regular quality audits.

7.2.1.4 Co-ordination

The Quality Manager shall:

- act as the focal point for all organisation quality matters within the organisation;

- co-ordinate and verify that all internal procedures and instructions are in accordance with the requirements of ISO 9001:2000 and the recommendations of ISO 9004:2000;
- operate the QMS as described in the Quality Manual and ensure that its regulations are observed.

Above all the Quality Manager must always ensure that the customer's interests are protected. Even if this means, at times, that he becomes very unpopular with the rest of the organisation and sometimes they even have to assume the mantel of organisation 'scapegoat'!

7.2.2   Chief Quality Assurance Inspector

Depending upon its size and activities, there may be more than one chief Quality Assurance Inspector (QAI) in an organisation.
The duties of the Chief QAI are to:

- plan, co-ordinate and supervise all pre-shop, in-process, and out-going inspections within their area of responsibility;
- ensure that the product is in agreement with the customers' requirements and conform to the established quality standards and specifications;
- be responsible for scheduling and controlling inspections, designating inspection stations, setting up local inspection procedures and statistical inspection controls;
- oversee the maintenance of inspection records, control charts and the preparation of inspection reports;
- ensure that all test equipment is maintained, properly calibrated and readily available at all inspection stations;
- be responsible for reviewing the maintenance of quality inspection stations;
- co-ordinate on-the-job and cross training within sections;
- establish and maintain inspection systems and controls to determine the acceptability of a completed product;
- be responsible for detecting deficiencies during manufacture, initiate corrective actions where applicable and prevent defects;
- compile quality and feedback data, quality history and statistical results to help quality control development, refinement and management;
- advise management and key maintenance personnel on all aspects concerning quality trends.

Within smaller organisations the role of Chief QAI is most likely to be taken on as part of the duties of a senior member of shop floor staff.

Managing Director

Quality Manager

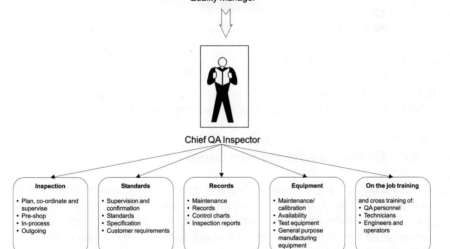

Chief QA Inspector

Inspection	Standards	Records	Equipment	On the job training
• Plan, co-ordinate and supervise • Pre-shop • In-process • Outgoing	• Supervision and confirmation • Standards • Specification • Customer requirements	• Maintenance • Records • Control charts • Inspection reports	• Maintenance/ calibration • Availability • Test equipment • General purpose manufacturing equipment	and cross training of: • QA personnel • Technicians • Engineers and operators

Figure 7.4 Responsibilities of the Chief Quality Assurance Inspector

7.2.3 Section Quality Assurance Inspectors

Two Section QAIs are normally nominated for each area, a principal and an alternate. The principal is always the Assurer, the alternate assumes the duties when asked to do so by the principal and during the absence of the principal. When not engaged on QA duties, the QAIs are employed on normal workshop activities.

The task of the section QAI is to:

● review (and make recommendations) to the chief QAI on all things concerning engineering change proposals, waivers, deviations and substitution of parts, materials, equipment and processes;

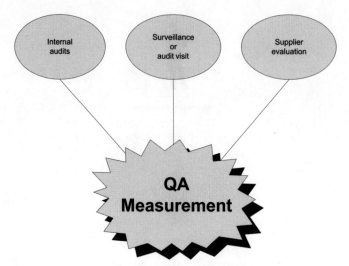

Figure 7.5 Responsibilities of the Section Quality Assurance Inspector

- compile quality feedback data and quality history sheets;
- supply technical data and assistance to the design office.

7.2.4   Quality Assurance personnel

Quality Assurance (QA) personnel are members of an organisation judged competent to carry out quality assurance duties. They are nominated by the Quality Manager in consultation with the QAIs and are directly responsible to the Quality Manager when engaged in QA work.
QA personnel are:

- not to allow their own judgement to be influenced by others;
- not to allow products (or services) to leave the premises below the desired standard;
- to ensure – by close liaison with section chiefs – that a section's work is not unreasonably delayed because of QA;
- to ensure that when a 'job' (i.e. service, system, module or equipment etc.) fails their inspection that the respective Section QAI is informed and that the section chief (and technician responsible) are made fully aware of the reasons for the failure;
- to advise the section quality assurance inspector of any problems associated with quality assurance, particularly anything that is likely to effect production or harmony between any of the sections and the quality assurance division.

7.2.5 The staff

Your staff are at the sharp end of delivering quality. They are responsible for implementing the quality control processes (i.e. the Work Instructions (WIs) see Section 2.7, p. 44.) that will ensure the desired level of quality is consistently applied to the product. Of course they are not responsible for setting the level of quality but, so long as they have been clearly briefed on what is required and have received the appropriate training to do the job, they will be capable of delivering that level of quality.

It is vital that a workforce is as committed to quality as the management. A committed workforce will look after your organisation. A workforce who is empowered to implement quality (and are allowed to have an input into defining and improving it) will be highly motivated. Morale will improve as staff will feel that they are doing a good job that they can be proud of.

In summary, an organisation's workforce has the responsibility for:

- working in accordance with the predefined WIs;
- refusing to accept anything that is substandard;
- having an active role in quality improvements;
- having an input into defining levels of quality (after all, they know better than anybody what can be achieved);
- delivering the level of quality specified in the QMS.

In short, your staff are your greatest asset.

Figure 7.6 Make sure you look after your staff!

7.3 Quality Assurance resources

It is not enough for management to supply just the personnel for a QA section. Resources, appropriate for the implementation of the quality policies, must also be available.

These shall include:

- management budget;
- training budget;
- design and development equipment;
- manufacturing equipment;
- inspection, test and examination equipment;
- instrumentation and computer software.

8 WHAT ARE THE PURCHASER'S RESPONSIBILITIES?

Quite a number of problems associated with a product's quality are usually the fault of the purchaser! Obviously the purchaser can only expect to get what he ordered. It is, therefore, extremely important that the actual order is not only correct, but also provides the manufacturer or service provider with all the relevant (and accurate) information required to complete the task.

There is little point in trying to blame the manufacturer or service provider when the finished product doesn't come up to expectation because of an unsatisfactory design provided by the purchaser. In certain cases (for example when the requirements of the item cannot easily be described in words), it could be very helpful if the purchaser was to provide a drawing as a form of graphic order. In such cases, this drawing should contain all the relevant details such as type of material to be used, the material's grade or condition, the specifications that are to be followed and, where possible, the graphic order/drawing should be to scale.

Figure 8.1 Insufficient information from the purchaser!

Figure 8.2 A good specification provided by the purchaser

If this approach proves impractical, then the order would have to include all the relevant dimensional data, sizes, tolerances etc., or refer to one of the accepted standards.

Having said all that, it must be appreciated that the actual specification being used is also very important for it sets the level of quality required and, therefore, directly affects the price of the article. Clearly, if specifications are too demanding then the final cost of the article will be too high. If specifications are too vague or obscure, then the manufacturer will have difficulty in assembling the object or may even be unable to get it to work correctly.

The choice of manufacturer or supplier of a service is equally important. It is an unfortunate fact of life that purchasers usually consider that the price of the article is the prime and (in some cases), even the only consideration. Buying cheaply is obviously **not** the answer because if a purchaser accepts the lowest offer all too often he will find that delivery times are lengthened (because the manufacturer/supplier can make more profit on other orders), the article produced does not satisfy his requirements and worst of all, the quality of the article is so poor that he has to replace the device well before its anticipated life cycle has been completed.

If a manufacturer or service provider has received official recognition that the quality of his work is up to a particular standard, then the purchaser has a reasonable guarantee that the article being produced will be of a reasonable quality – always assuming that the initial order was correct! Official recognition is taken to mean that an organisation has been assessed and certified to a recognised quality standard such as ISO 9000. In other words he can **prove** his level of quality.

9 WHAT ARE THE SUPPLIER'S RESPONSIBILITIES?

The term 'supplier' normally relates to organisations that manufacture goods **or** provide services. The suppliers prime responsibility must always be to ensure that anything **and everything** leaving their organisation conforms to the specific requirements of the purchaser – particularly with regard to quality.

The simplest way of doing this is for the supplier to ensure that their particular office, production facility or manufacturing/service outlet fully complies with the requirements of the quality standards adopted by the country in which they are manufacturing and the country to whom they intend supplying the component, equipment or system.

To do this they must of course first be aware of the standards applicable to that country, know how to obtain copies of these standards, how to adapt them to their own particular environment and how to get them accepted by the relevant authorities.

Every country has its own set of recognised quality management standards to which suppliers can be assessed and certified. Table 9.1 indicates the most frequently used certification and guideline standards used within the UK.

Although a firm can set out to abide by accepted standards, however, unless they achieve this aim they will fail in their attempt to become a recognised supplier of quality goods. The main points that they should note are:

- that all managerial staff, from the most junior to the most senior, must firmly believe in the importance of quality control and quality assurance and understand how to implement them;
- that managerial staff **must** create an atmosphere in which quality assurance rules are obeyed and not simply avoided just because they are inconvenient, time consuming, laborious or just too boring to bother with;

Table 9.1 Certification and guideline standards

Certification Standards	Description	Guideline Standards	Description
ISO 9001: 2000	Model for quality assurance requirements in design, development, production, installation and servicing	ISO 9004: 2000	Quality management and quality system guidance
ISO 14001: 1996	Requirements for an environmental management system ensuring continual improvement	BS 7799: 1995	Information security management system recommendations
Investors in People	Model for human resources, with special emphasis on management system requirements for training		

- that there has to be an accepted training scheme to ensure that all members of the firm are regularly brought up to date with the ongoing and the latest requirements of quality assurance;
- that there must be a quality assurance team available to oversee and make sure that quality control and quality assurance are carried out at all times and **at all levels**, within their premises.

Figure 9.1 If you've got it, flaunt it!

In addition, the supplier will have to provide proof that they are supplying a quality product. This is actually a measurement of their quality control and usually takes the form of a suppliers evaluation, surveillance and audit. The evaluation is carried out by:

- the prospective purchaser of the product, or
- an accredited body (such as Lloyd's, BSI or SGS etc.) which, if successful, will allow the supplier to proudly display a compliance certificate and to use the recognised quality mark on their stationery and marketing literature.

Abbreviations and Acronyms

ACE	Allied Command Europe
AECMA	Association Europeen des Constructeurs de Materiel Aerospatial
AFNOR	Association Français de Normalisation
AMIQA	Associate Member of the Institute of Quality Assurance
ANSI	American National Standards Institute
AQAP	Allied Quality Assurance Publications (NATO)
AS 9000	Quality system standard for the aerospace industry, issued by SAE (USA)
ASQ	American Society for Quality (was ASQC)
ASQC	American Society for Quality Control (now ASQ)
BEC	British Electro-Technical Committee (part of BSI)
BS	British Standard, issued by BSI
BSI	British Standards Institution
CASCO	Committee for Conformity Assessment
CCA	Accord de Certification du CENELEC (CENELEC Certification Agreement)
CCIR	International Radio Consultative Committee
CCITT	The International Telegraph and Telephony Consultative Committee
CD	Committee Draft
CECC	CENELEC Electronic Components Committee
CEE	International Commission on rules for the approval of Electrical Equipment (now mostly replaced by IEC publications)
CEN	Commission European de Normalisation
CENELEC	European Committee for Electrotechnical Standardisation
COMSEC	Communications Security
CSA	Canadian Standards Association
DEF	Defence Standard (UK)
Def Spec	Defence Specification (UK)
DEF STAN	Defence Standards (UK)

DIN	Deutsches Institut für Normung (German Institute for Standardisation)
DIS	Draft International Standard
DTI	Department of Trade and Industry
DOD	(American) Division of Defence
EEC	European Economic Community
EFQM	European Foundation for Quality Management
EFTA	European Free Trade Association (Iceland, Norway, Switzerland and Liechtenstein)
EN	European Number (for European standards)
EN HD	European Harmonised Directive
EOQ	European Organisation for Quality
EOQC	European Organisation for Quality Control (now EOQ)
EQFM	European Foundation of Quality Management
ERRI	European Rail Research Institute
ERTMS	European Rail Traffic Management System
ETCS	European Train Control System
ETSI	European Telecommunications Standards Institute
EU	European Union
FDIS	Final Draft International Standard
FIIE(elec)	Fellow of the Institution of Electronics and Electrical Incorporated Engineers
FinstM	Fellow of the Institute of Management
IAF	International Accreditation Forum
IEC	International Electrotechnical Commission
IECC	International Electrotechnical Commission Council
IECQ	IEC Quality Assessment System for Electronic Components
IEE	Institution of Electrical Engineers
IQA	Institute of Quality Assurance
ISO	International Organisation for Standardisation
ISO/TC176	The ISO Technical Committee responsible for the ISO 9000 series of standards.
IT	Information Technology
ITU	International Telecommunications Union
JPL	Jet Propulsion Laboratory
LAN	Local Area Network
Mil-Spec	Military Specification (USA)
Mil-Std	Military Standard (USA)

MIQA	Member of the Institute of Quality Assurance
MIRSE	Member of the Institution of Railway Signal Engineers
MOD	Ministry of Defence
MSc	Master of Science

NASA	National Aeronautics and Space Administration
NATO	North Atlantic Treaty Organisation
NSA	National Supervising Authority
NSOQA	National Standards Organisation

QAI	Quality Assurance Inspector
QC	Quality Control
QMS	Quality Management System
QP	Quality Procedure
QS	(automotive standard)
QT	(telecomms standard)

| RAMS | Reliability, Availability, Maintenance and Safety |

| SIS | Swedish Institute for Standards |

TC	Technical Committee
TQM	Total Quality Management (e.g. BS 7850)
TTCI	Transportation Technology Center Inc

| UIC | Union International des Chemins de fer |
| UK | United Kingdom |

| VDE | Verband Deutsch Elektrotechniker |

| WD | Working Draft |
| WI | Work Instruction |

REFERENCES

Standards

Number	Date	Title
93/42/EEC	1993	European Community Council Directive concerning medical devices
ANSI 90 series		American quality standards
BS 0	1997	A standard for standards – Guide to the context, aims and general principles
BS 0:PT1	1991	A standard for standards – Guide to general principles of standardisation
BS 0:PT2	1991	A standard for standards – BSI and its committee procedures
BS 0:PT3	1991	A standard for standards – Guide to drafting and presentation of British Standards
BS 3934	1965	Specification for the dimensions of semiconductor devices and integrated electronic circuits
BS 4778	1979	Quality vocabulary
BS 4891	1972	A Guide to Quality Assurance
BS 5750 series	1987	Quality systems – Principal concepts and applications
BS 5750: PT1	1979	Quality systems – Specification for design, development, production, installation and servicing

Number	Date	Title
BS 5750: PT2	1979	Quality systems – Specification for production and installation
BS 5750: PT3	1979	Quality systems – Specification for final inspection and test
BS 8800	1996	Guide to occupational health and safety management systems
DEF STAN 13–131/2	1997	Ordnance Board safety guidelines for weapons and munitions
DIS ISO 9000	1999	Quality management systems – Fundaments and vocabulary
DIS ISO 9001	1999	Quality management systems – Requirements
DIS ISO 9004	1999	Quality management systems – Guidance for performance improvement
EN 29000	1987	Renumbered as ISO 9000/1
ISO 8402	1995	Quality management and quality assurance – Vocabulary
ISO 9000		Quality management and quality assurance standards
ISO 9000	2000	Quality management systems – Fundaments and vocabulary
ISO 9000/1	1994	Quality management and quality assurance standards – Guidelines for selection and use
ISO 9000/2	1997	Quality management and quality assurance standards – Generic guidelines for the application of ISO 9001, 9002 and 9003
ISO 9000/3	1997	Quality management and quality assurance standards – Guidelines for the application of ISO 9001:1994 to the development, supply, installation and maintenance of computer software
ISO 9000/4	1993	Quality management and quality assurance standards – Guide to dependability programme management

Number	Date	Title
ISO 9001	1994	Quality systems – Model for quality assurance in design/development, production, installation and servicing
ISO 9001	2000	Quality management systems – Requirements
ISO 9002	1994	Quality systems – Model for quality assurance in production and installation
ISO 9003	1994	Quality systems – Model for quality assurance in final inspection and test
ISO 9004	1987	Superseded by ISO 9004/1
ISO 9004	2000	Quality management systems – Guidance for performance improvement
ISO 9004/1	1994	Quality management and quality system elements – Guidelines
ISO 9004/2	1991	Quality management and quality system elements – Guidelines for service
ISO 9004/3	1993	Quality management and quality system elements – Guidelines for processed materials
ISO 9004/4	1994	Quality management and quality system elements – Guidelines for quality improvement
ISO 10005	1995	Quality management – Guidelines for quality plans
ISO 10011/1	1990	Guidelines for auditing quality systems – Auditing
ISO 10011/2	1991	Guidelines for auditing quality systems – Qualification criteria for quality systems auditors
ISO 10011/3	1991	Guidelines for auditing quality systems – Management of audit programmes
ISO 10012/1	1992	Quality assurance requirements for measuring equipment – Metrological confirmation system for measuring equipment

Number	Date	Title
ISO 10012/2	1997	Quality assurance for measuring equipment – Guidelines for control of measurement processes
ISO 10013	1995	Guidelines for developing quality manuals
ISO 14001	1996	Environmental management systems – Specifications with guidance for use
ISO 14010	1996	Guidelines for environmental auditing – General principles
ISO 14011	1996	Guidelines for environmental auditing – Auditing procedures – Auditing of environmental management systems
ISO 14012	1996	Guidelines for environmental auditing – Qualification criteria for environmental auditors
QS 9000	1995	Quality system requirements (for the automotive industry)
TR 9000		Quality system requirements (for the electronics industry)

NOTES

Extracts from British Standards are reproduced with the permission of the British Standards Institute. Complete copies of all British Standards can be obtained, by post, from Customer Services, BSI Standards, 389 Chiswick High Road, London W4 4AL.

Books by the same author

Title	Details	Publisher
Quality and Standards in Electronics	Ensures that manufacturers are aware of the all the UK, European and international necessities, know the current status of these regulations and standards, and where to obtain them.	Butterworth-Heinemann ISBN: 0 7506 2531 7

Title	Details	Publisher
Environmental Requirements for Electromechanical and Electronic Equipment	Definitive reference containing all the background guidance, ranges, test specifications, case studies and regulations worldwide.	Butterworth-Heinemann ISBN: 0 7506 3902 4
MDD Compliance using Quality Management Techniques	Easy to follow guide to MDD, enabling purchaser to customise the Quality Management System to suit his own business.	Butterworth-Heinemann ISBN: 0 7506 4441 9
CE Conformity Marking	Essential information for any manufacturer or distributor wishing to trade in the EU.	Butterworth-Heinemann ISBN: 0 7506 4813 9
ISO 9001:2000 for Small Businesses	Explains the importance of ISO 9001:2000, the ISO 9000:2000 family and helps businesses draw up a quality plan that will allow them to meet the challenges of the marketplace.	Butterworth-Heinemann ISBN: 0 7506 4882 1

GLOSSARY

Acceptable quality level: A measure of the number of failures that a production process is allowed. Usually expressed as a percentage.

Accreditation: Certification, by a duly recognised body, of facilities, capability, objectivity, competence and integrity of an agency, service or operational group or individual to provide the specific service/s or operation/s as needed.

Assemblies: Several pieces of equipment assembled by a manufacturer to constitute an integrated and functional whole.

Audit: Systematic, independent and documented process for obtaining evidence and evaluating it objectively to determine the extent to which audit criteria are fulfilled.

Audit team: One or more auditors conducting an audit, one of whom is appointed as leader.

CEN (European Committee for Standardisation): European equivalent of ISO.

CENELEC (European Committee for Electrotechnical Standardisation) certification body: An impartial body who have the necessary competence and reliability to operate a certification scheme.

Certification: The procedure and action by a duly authorised body of determining, verifying and attesting in writing to the qualifications of personnel, processes, procedures, or items in accordance with applicable requirements.

Certification body: An impartial body, governmental or non-governmental, possessing the necessary competence and reliability to operate a certification system, and in which the interests of all parties concerned with the functioning of the system are represented. An impartial body

who have the necessary competence and reliability to operate a certification scheme.

Chief inspector: An individual who is responsible for the manufacturer's Quality Management System (also referred to as the Quality Manager).

Company: Term used primarily to refer to a business first party, the purpose of which is to supply a product or service.

Compliance: An affirmative indication or judgement that a product or service has met the requirements of the relevant specifications, contract or regulation. Also the state of meeting the requirements.

Conformance: An affirmative indication or judgement that a product or service has met the requirements of the relevant specifications, contract or regulation. Also the state of meeting the requirements.

Contract: Agreed requirements between a supplier and customer transmitted by any means.

Customer: Ultimate consumer, user, client, beneficiary or second party.

Customer satisfaction: Customer's opinion of the degree to which a transaction has met the customer's needs and expectations.

Defect: Non-fulfilment of a requirement related to an intended or specified use.

Design and development: Set of processes that transforms requirements into specified characteristics and into the specification of the product realisation process.

Distributor: An organisation that is contractually authorised by one or more manufacturers to store, repack and sell completely finished components from these manufacturers.

Document: Information and its support medium.

Environment: All of the external physical conditions that may influence the performance of a product or service.

Equipment: Machines, apparatus, fixed or mobile devices, control components and instrumentation thereof and detection or prevention systems which, separately or jointly, are intended for the generation, transfer, storage, measurement, control and conversion of energy for the processing of material and which are capable of causing an explosion through their own potential sources of ignition.

External failure costs: The costs arising outside an organisation after the delivery to customer/user due to failure to fulfil the customer/user quality requirements.

In-process inspection: Inspection carried out at various stages during processing.

QA Inspectors perform these on a random basis or while assisting the technician. They may also be considered as 'Training' inspections and are meant to help the technician perform better maintenance whilst actually learning about the equipment.

International Organisation for Standardisation (ISO): Comprises the national standards bodies of more than 50 countries whose aim is to co-ordinate the international harmonisation of national standards.

Item: A part, a component, equipment, sub-system or system or defined quantity of material or service that can be individually considered and separately examined or tested.

An actual or conventional object on which a set of observations can be made.

An observed value, either qualitative (attributes) or quantitative (measured).

Maintenance: The combination of technical and administrative actions that are taken to retain or restore an item to a state in which it can perform its stated function.

Management: Co-ordinated activities to direct and control an organisation.

Management system: To establish policy and objectives and to achieve those objectives.

Manufacturer: An organisation, which carries out or controls such stages in the manufacture of electronic components that enable it to accept responsibility for capability approval or qualification approval, inspection and release of electronic components.

Material: A generic term covering equipment, stores, supplies and spares which form the subject of a contract.

Non-conformity: Non-fulfilment of a requirement.

Organisation: Group of people and facilities with an orderly arrangement of responsibilities, authorities and relationships.

A company, corporation, firm or enterprise, whether incorporated or not, public or private.

Organisational structure: Orderly arrangement of responsibilities, authorities and relationships between people.

Procedure: Describes the way to perform an activity or process.

Process inspection: Inspection of a process by examination of the process itself, the product characteristics at the appropriate stage(s) of the process.

Producer's quality costs: The expenditure incurred by the producer associated with prevention and appraisal activities and with the failure to achieve quality requirements during marketing, design and development, procurement, manufacturing, installation and use.

Product: Result of a process.
  Note: There are four agreed generic product categories:

- hardware (e.g. engine mechanical part);
- software (e.g. computer program);
- services (e.g. transport);
- processed materials (e.g. lubricant).

Hardware and processed materials are generally tangible products, while software or services are generally intangible.

Most products comprise elements belonging to different generic product categories. Whether the product is then called hardware, processed material, software or service depends on the dominant element.

Project: Unique process, consisting of a set of co-ordinated and controlled activities with start and finish dates, undertaken to achieve an objective conforming to specific requirements, including the constraints of time, costs and resources.

Quality: Ability of a set of inherent characteristics of a product, system or process to fulfil requirements of customers and other interested parties.
  The totality of features and characteristics of a product or service that bear upon its ability to satisfy stated or implied needs.

Quality Assurance: Part of quality management, focused on providing confidence that quality requirements are fulfilled.

Quality characteristic: Inherent characteristic of a product, process or system derived from a requirement.

Quality Control: The operational techniques and activities that are used to fulfil requirements for quality.

Quality costs: The expenditure incurred by the producer, by the user and by the community, associated with product or service quality.

Quality level: A measure of quality expressed in terms of a quantitative value such as proportion effective, percent non-conforming, parts per million, etc.

Quality loop: Conceptual model of interacting activities that influence the quality of a product or service in the various stages ranging from the identification of needs to the assessment of whether these needs have been satisfied.

Quality Manager: A person who is responsible for the manufacturer's Quality Management System (also sometimes referred to as the Chief Inspector).

Quality management: That aspect of the overall management function that determines and implements the quality policy.

   Note: The terms 'Quality Management' and 'Quality Control' are considered to be a manufacturer/supplier (or 1st party) responsibility. 'Quality Assurance' on the other hand has both internal and external aspects which in many instances can be shared between the manufacturer/supplier (1st party), purchaser/customer (2nd party) and any regulatory/certification body (3rd party) that may be involved.

Quality Management System: System to establish a quality policy and quality objectives and to achieve those objectives.

Quality Management System review: A formal evaluation by top management of the status and adequacy of the Quality Management System in relation to quality policy and new objectives resulting from changing circumstances.

Quality Manual: Document specifying the quality management system of an organisation and setting out the quality policies, systems and practices of an organisation.

Quality Plan: Document specifying the quality management system elements and the resources to be applied in a specific case.

Quality planning: Part of quality management focused on setting quality objectives and specifying necessary operational processes and related resources to fulfil the quality objectives.

Quality Policy: The overall quality intentions and direction of an organisation as regards quality, as formally expressed by top management.

Quality Procedure: A description of the method by which quality system activities are managed.

Quality records: Records should provide evidence of how well the Quality System has been implemented.

Quality system: The organisational structure, responsibilities, procedures, processes and resources for implementing quality management.

Quality system review: A formal evaluation by top management of the status and adequacy of the quality system in relation to quality policy and new objectives resulting from changing circumstances.

Record: Document stating results achieved or providing evidence of activities performed.

Requirement: Need or expectation that is stated, customarily implied or obligatory.

Review: Activity undertaken to ensure the suitability, adequacy, effectiveness and efficiency of the subject matter to achieve established objectives.

Service: Intangible product that is the result of at least one activity performed at the interface between the supplier and customer
  Note: Service may involve, for example:

- an activity performed on a customer-supplied tangible (e.g. the repair of a car) or intangible (e.g. the preparation of a tax return) product;
- the delivery of a tangible product (2A.2) (e.g. in the transportation industry);
- the delivery of an intangible product (e.g. the delivery of knowledge) or the creation of ambience for the customer (e.g. in the hospitality industry).

Shall: This auxiliary verb indicates that a certain course of action is mandatory.

Should: This auxiliary verb indicates that a certain course of action is preferred but not necessarily required.

Supplier: The organisation that provides a product to the customer [EN ISO 8402:1995].

Note 1. In a contractual situation, the supplier may be called the contractor.
Note 2. The supplier may be, for example, the producer, distributor, importer, assembler or service organisation.
Note 3. The supplier may be either external or internal to the organisation.
Note 4. With regard to MDD the term Supplier is *not* used. The Directive instead refers to 'manufacturer'.

Top management: Person or group of people who direct and control an organisation at the highest level.

Work Instruction: A description of how a specific task is carried out.

Useful addresses

American National Standards Institute (ANSI)

1819 L Street, NW
Washington, DC 20036, USA
Tel: 00 1 202 293 8020
Fax: 00 1 202 293 9287
e-mail: **ansionline@ansi.org**
website: **http://www.ansi.org**

American Society for Quality Control (ASQ)

611 East Wisconsin Avenue
P. O. Box 3005
Milwaukee WI 53201–3005, USA
Tel: 00 1 414 272 8575 or 800 248 1946
Fax: 00 1 414 272 1734
e-mail: **cs@asq.org**
website: **http://www.asq.org**

Asociación Española de Normalización y Certificación (AENOR)

Génova 6
28004 Madrid, Spain
Tel: 0034 914 32 60 00 – 4 32 60 23
  (Info Service)
Fax: 0034 913 10 45 96 - 3 10 36 95
  (Stand Dept)
e-mail: **norm.clciec@aenor.es**
website: **http://www.aenor.es**

British Electrotechnical Committee (BEC)

See British Standards Institution (BSI)

British Standards Institution (BSI)

389 Chiswick High Road
London W4 4AL, UK
Tel: 020 8996 9001
Fax: 020 8996 7001
e-mail: **info@bsi.org.uk**
website: **http://www.bsi.org.uk**

Comission Europeen de Normalisation (CEN)

36, rue de Stassart
1050 Bruxelles, Belgium
Tel: 0032 2 550 08 11
Fax: 0032 2 550 08 19
e-mail: **infodesk@cenclcbel.be**
website: **http://www.cenorm.be**

Comitato Elettrotecnico Italiano (CEI)

Viale Monza 261
20126 Milano, Italy
Tel: 0039 02 25 77 3 226
Fax: 0039 02 25 77 3 210
e-mail: **cei@ceiuni.it**
website: **http://www.ceiuni.it**

Comité Electrotechnique Belge (CEB) Belgisch Elektrotechnisch Comité (BEC)

Boulevard A Reyerslaan 80
1030 Bruxelles, Belgium
Tel: 0032 2 706 8570
Fax: 0032 2 556 01 20
e-mail: **centraloffice@bec-ceb.be**
website: **http://www.bec-ceb.be**

Czech Standards Institute(CSNI)

Biskupsky dvůr 5
110 02 Praha 1, Czech Republic
Tel: 00 420 2 21 80 21 11
Fax: 00 420 2 21 80 23 01
e-mail: **csni@login.cz**
website: **http://www.csni.cz**

Dansk Standard (DS) Electrotechnical Sector

Kollegievej 6
2920 Charlottenlund, Denmark
Tel: 0045 39 96 61 01
Fax: 0045 39 96 61 02
Fax: 0045 39 96 61 03
   (Certification dept.)
e-mail: **standard@ds.dk**
website: **http://www.ds.dk**

Deutsche Elektrotechnische Kommission im DIN und VDE (DKE)

Stresemannallee 15
D – 60596 Frankfurt am Main, Germany
Tel: 0049 69 63 080
Fax: 0049 69 63 12 925
e-mail: **dke.zbt@t-online.de**
website: **http://www.dke.de**

Electro-Technical Council of Ireland (ETCI)	Unit 43 Parkwest Business Park Dublin 12, Ireland Tel: 00353 1 623 9901 Fax: 00353 1 623 9903 e-mail: **administrator@etci.ie** website: **http://www.etci.ie**
European Telecommunications Standards Institution (ETSI)	Route des Lucioles – Sophia Antipolis – Valbonne 06921 Sophia Antipolis, France Tel: 0033 4 92 94 42 00 Fax : 0033 4 93 65 47 16 e-mail: **infocentre@etsi.fr** website: **http://www.etsi.org**
European Committee for Electrotechnical Standardisation (CENELEC)	35, rue de Stassart 1050 Bruxelles, Belgium Tel: 0032 2 519 68 71 Fax : 0032 2 519 69 19 e-mail: **general@cenelec.be** website: **http://www.cenelec.be**
Finnish Electrotechnical Standards Association (SESKO)	Särkiniementie 3 PL 134 00211 Helsinki, Finland Tel: 00358 9 696 391 Fax: 00358 9 677 059 e-mail: **finc@sesko.fi** website: **http://www.sesko.fi**
Hellenic Organization for Standardization (ELOT)	Acharnon Street 313 111 45 Athens, Greece Tel: 0030 1 212 01 00 Fax: 0030 1 228 30 34 e-mail: **elotinfo@elot.gr** website: **http://www.elot.gr**
Infonorme London Information (ILI)	Index House Ascot Berkshire SL5 7EU, UK Tel: 01344 636400 Fax: 01344 291194 e-mail: **databases@ili.co.uk** website: **www.ili.co.uk**

ILI (America)	60 Winters Avenue Paramus, NJ 07652, USA e-mail: **sales@ili-info.com**
Instituto Português da Qualidade (IPQ)	Rua Antorio Ciao 2 2829–513 Caparica, Portugal Tel: 00351 1 294 81 00 Fax: 00351 1 294 81 81 e-mail: **ipq@mail.ipq.pt** website: **http://www.ipq.pt**
International Electrotechnical Commission (IEC)	Rue de Varembe 3 Case Postale 131 1211 Geneva 20, Switzerland Tel: 0041 22 919 0211 Fax: 0041 22 919 0300 website: **http://www.iec.ch**
International Standards Organisation (ISO)	Case Postal 56 1222 Geneva 20, Switzerland Tel: 0041 22 749 0336 Fax: 0041 22 734 1079 website: **http://www.iso.ch**
National Center for Standards and Certification Information	US Department of Commerce Building 820, Room 164 Gaithersburg, MD 20899, USA Tel: 00 1 301 9754040 EU Hotline: 00 1 301 921–4164 Fax: 00 1 301 926 1559
Nederlands Elektrotechnisch Comité (NEC)	Kalfjeslaan 2 Postbus 5059 2600 GB Delft, The Netherlands Tel: 0031 15 269 03 90 Fax: 0031 15 269 01 90 e-mail: **info@nni.nl** website: **http://www.nni.nl**
Norsk Elektroteknisk Komite (NEK)	Harbitzalléen 2A Postboks 280 Skoyen N – 0212 Oslo, Norway Tel: 0047 22 52 69 50 Fax: 0047 22 52 69 61 e-mail: **nek@nek.no** website: **http://www.nek.no**

Office of the European Union And Regulatory Affairs	US Dept of Commerce – Room 3036 14th & Constitution Avenue, N.W. Washington, D.C. 20230 Tel: 00 1 202 482 5276 Fax: 001 202482 2155
Office of the Official Publications of the EC	2 Rue Mercier 2144 Luxembourg Tel: 00352–29291 Fax: 00352 292942763 e-mail: **infor.info@opece.cec.be** website: **http://www.eur-op.eu.int**
Österreichisches Elektrotechnisches Komitee (ÖEK) Österreichischen Verband für Elektrotechnik (ÖVE)	Eschenbachgasse 9 1010 Vienna, Austria Tel: 0043 1 587 63 73 Fax: 0043 1 586 74 08 e-mail: **ove@ove.at** website: **http://www.ove.at**
Service de l'Energie de l'Etat (SEE)	B.P. 10 2010 Luxembourg Tel: 00352 46 97 461 Fax: 00352 46 97 46 – 39 e-mail: **see.normalisation@eg.etat.lu** website: **http://www.etat.lu/SEE**
Svenska Elektriska Kommissionen (SEK)	Kistagången 19 Box 1284 64 29 Kista Stockholm, Sweden Tel: 0046 8 444 14 00 Fax: 0046 8 444 14 30 e-mail: **snc@sekom.se** website: **http://www.sekom.se**
Swiss Electrotechnical Committee (CES)	Luppmenstraße 1 8320 Fehraltorf, Switzerland Tel: 0041 1 956 11 11 Fax: 00 41 1 956 11 22 e-mail: **sev@sev.ch** website: **http://www.sev.ch**
The Icelandic Council for Standardization (STRI)	Holtagardar 104 Reykjavik, Iceland Tel: 00354 520 71 50 Fax: 00354 520 71 71 e-mail: **stri@stri.is** website: **http://www.stri.is**

Union Technique de
l'Electricité (UTE)

33, Av. Général Leclerc - BP 23
F – 92262 Fontenay-aux-Roses, France
Tel: 0033 1 40 93 62 00
Fax: 0033 1 40 93 44 08
e-mail: **ute@ute.asso.fr**
website: **http://www.ute-fr.com**

VDE-Verlag GmbH

Bismarkstrasse 33
10625 Berlin, Germany
Tel: 0049 30 348001–0
Fax: 0049 30 3417093
e-mail: **service@vde.com**
website: **http://www.vde.de**

Index